THE WARRIOR LORD'S TRIUMPH

The Warrior Lord's Triumph

Published by Ray and Mary Hawkins
© Ray Hawkins 2017
Tasmania, Australia
www.mary-hawkins.com
http://rayhawkinsauthor.blogspot.com.au

Design and layout by Book Whispers

National Library of Australia Cataloguing-in-Publication entry

Creator: Hawkins, Ray, author.
Title: The warrior lord's triumph / Ray Hawkins.
ISBN: 9780994539427 (paperback)
Subjects: Jesus Christ--Resurrection.
Jesus Christ--Promises.
Jesus Christ--Prophecies.
Second Advent.

Devotional literature. All rights reserved. No part of this publication may be reproduced, stored in, or introduced into a retrieval system, or transmitted, in any form, or by any means (electronic, mechanical, photocopying, recording or otherwise) without the prior written permission of the publisher.

Unless otherwise indicated all Bible quotes are from the New Revised Standard Version and New King James Version.

THE WARRIOR LORD'S TRIUMPH

Ray Hawkins

http://rayhawkinsauthor.blogspot.com.au

Contents

Foreword	viii
Introduction	1
Maranatha	3
The Meeting in the Air	5
As a Thief He comes	7
Why God Laughs	9
The Dark City's Overthrow	11
The Day of God's Jealousy	13
Back in Residence	15
Reflection/Study#1.	17
Preparing for the Return.	18
As in the Day of Noah	20
Being Confident when He Comes	22
The Three in One Shepherd	24
Heaven's Hallelujah Chorus	26
A Forgotten Reason	28
The Dream, the Idol and the Stone	30
Reflection/study #2	32
God Clear Purpose	33
Insights into the Thousand Year Reign	36
The Parousia of Christ	38
The Apocalypse of Christ	40

The Hill of the Lord	42
When God Sings Solo	44
Sheep, Goats and the King	46
Reflections/study #3.	48
The Judgement Seat of Christ	49
Behold 'The Lamb'	51
Heralds of Apostasy	53
Jerusalem, no longer Forsaken	56
The Epiphany of Christ	58
The Chariots of Clouds	60
Universal Restoration Begun	62
Reflection/Study#4	64
Clues to Christ's Return	65
Eyes of Fire	67
All Things New	69
Reflection/study #5	71

Introduction
The Warrior King Returns.

These 31 days Devotional Meditations are selective. Each day wants to refresh your faith and defend your understanding of Christ's promised return. They seek to lift your spirits above the crushing despair caused by World events.

This isn't a systematic thesis explaining events or chronologies. There are many fine commentaries and specialist books dealing with such matters. Rather, as you read a segment each day for the month you will be more aware of where today's events are heading. Christ is faithful. His word is sure. Together they have left us with enough information about future events so that we can face the future with hope. In turn this will make us wise in our priorities and trustworthy in our relationships.

The teaching about the second coming of the Lord Jesus Christ is very explicit in Scripture. Whenever we share in Holy communion/the Lord's Supper/ Eucharist we proclaim this is only until 'He comes!' When we say the Lord's Prayer we acknowledge the fact of His return to set up the Kingdom of God. The fulfilment of Christ's victory on the cross can only be fully expressed by our Lord's visible, tangible and triumphant return to earth.

Jesus came as the Warrior Baby (see my 'Bethlehem's Warrior Baby'). In the battle for our salvation and deliverance from judgement He died on our behalf. His resurrection from the dead proclaimed Him Conqueror of Sin and Death. Jesus is now the believer's Lord, hero and advocate in Heaven. He waits the Father's designated time to return as the warrior Lord.

In the meantime our Lord empowers us by His Holy Spirit to be His ambassadors in enemy territory. We are His witnesses living out the wonder of His grace in our lives. For us to be found faithful to His word requires us to understand His will and purposes. We find them within the pages of Scripture.

These devotions are offered as a means of knowing Christ's heart and mind in relation to His promised return. May they thrill your heart and arouse an ever deepening love of our faithful and covenant keeping Lord. At the conclusion of each seven days there is an opportunity for personal reflection or group discussion.

Maranatha
Day1

Verse: 'If any man love not the Lord Jesus Christ, Let him be Anathema, Maranatha' 1 Corinthians 16:22. KJV.

When the Apostle Paul concluded 1st Corinthians you can almost feel the longing wrapped up in Maranatha. It is an Aramaic word meaning 'Lord come!' It is an ejaculatory outburst of deep longing and only used here. Paul had strategically placed mention of the Lord's return throughout Corinthians. It became a motivation for Christian living and service and also for worship. 1 Corinthians 1:7 '…as you wait for the revealing of our Lord Jesus Christ. He will also strengthen you to the end, so that you may be blameless on the day of our Lord Jesus Christ.' In the disciplining passage on worship and communion Paul reminds them they share in the Lord's Supper 'until he (Christ) comes.'

In the first century Church there was an expectation which is sadly lacking today. As you read the New Testament this longing reveals itself in many different ways. Christians lived in the hope of the imminent return of their Lord and Saviour. From Pentecost onwards disciples were instructed in the hope and doctrine of the second coming.

Maranatha flavours almost every epistle. For those enduring persecution this longing sustained them. We may or may not have similar experiences. However there is something in the heart of a follower of Christ which cries "Maranatha!" Why? For any number of reasons! We want to see Him. We want His Kingdom of righteousness and truth to be established. We long for His Name to be vindicated.

Some Christians are curious about why Jesus is taking so long to return. A study of Scripture presents you with a number of reasons for this. Among them are historical, political and spiritual features which must first come together. Peter also highlights a very important aspect, 'The Lord is not slow about his promise, as some think of slowness, but is patient with you, not wanting any to perish, but all to come to repentance' (2 Peter3:9).

God hasn't ignored the Church's cry. He is moving prophecy into place piece by piece. The World will be in no doubt who is Sovereign when things foretold begin to happen. This is part of the reason for God's foretelling of events. As is said many times in the book of Ezekiel, when they come to pass, "Then you shall know that I am the Lord". Jesus told His followers to look forward to this, 'Now when these things begin to take place, stand up and raise your heads, because your redemption is drawing near' (Luke 21:28).

In both the Testaments you will find matters still outstanding. At the moment they may appear impossible or ridiculous. Don't be depressed by the sceptics: they said the same about the first coming of Jesus. Christmas, Calvary and Christ's resurrection proved the sceptics wrong. In the fullness of time Christ Jesus came (Galatians 4:4). His return is also predicated upon the same premise. Christians longing for 'Maranatha' actually face a dilemma. They know that the longing of their heart is preceded by tough times. The prophets have said it. So too the apostles. Jesus taught it (Luke 21:8-19). The longing however is so strong that Christ's people still declare "though the times be unpleasant, unfair and unwanted I will stand true to my Lord and Saviour. Every pressure brought to bear simply makes me cry out all the more 'Maranatha! O Lord, come!'"

Habakkuk's words relating to another matter are relevant for us today. 'The Lord answered me and said: Write the vision; make it plain on tablets, so that a runner may read it. For there is still a vision for the appointed time; it speaks of the end, and does not lie. If it seems to tarry, wait for it; it will surely come, it will not delay' (Habakkuk 2:2-3). Until then our longing remains…

Maranatha!

The Meeting in the Air
Day 2.

Verse: 'The Lord himself, with a cry of command, with the archangel's call and with the sound of God's trumpet, will descend from heaven, and the dead in Christ will rise first. Then we who are alive, who are left, will be caught up in the clouds together with them to meet the Lord in the air; and so we will be with the Lord forever.' 1Thessalonians 4:16-17

Those who long for the second coming of Christ could be confused by various theories about the event. One confusion arises from either mixing Israel and the Church or holding to the view that God has finished with that Nation. Problems arise for a proper understanding of Christ's return if there isn't a clear distinction between Israel and the Church. The Nation was promised the land and the Messiah as king. The Church is International with a spiritual Body and Christ as Its Head. To wipe out the nation from any further usefulness to God undermines and disparages Old Testament prophecies.

The second coming of Jesus is centred upon the nation of Israel! That nation is now spiritually blind through unbelief and hardness of heart towards Jesus as their Messiah. Jesus looked forward to the day when the nation would have its eyes opened (Matthew 23:39). We must remember when Jesus spoke about His return the Church was not yet conceived. His teachings were to and about Israel. The Church is God's surprise. It is the mystery which God kept hidden [Ephesians 3. Romans 16:25-27] until the Nation of Israel turned its back on Jesus. Therefore, this raises a question: what is the destiny of the Church and the future of Israel?

When the Church hears the trumpet sound.

The key passages for this are 1 Thessalonians 4:13-5:11 and 1 Corinthians 15. Believers in Thessalonica were concerned about those Christians who died before Christ's return. They had been expecting His appearing in a very short space of time but some of their number had died. What would happen to them? Would they miss out? In response, Paul outlined for them the wonderful hope of the Church. Christ Jesus calls the believers, dead or alive, to meet Him in the air. Three features mark this time out:

a. *'A cry of command' is a general's command to his soldiers or an Admiral's to his oarsmen.*
b. *'The archangel's call' will wake the dead, and presumably frighten the ungodly. From other Scripture when the angels shout they do it loudly.*
c. *'God's trumpet' will reverberate with its battle sound.*

No silent rapture is envisaged from those words.

Those believers asleep in the grave rise first, then those believers still alive are 'caught up,' to an assembly in the air. This word for 'caught up' is used 12 times in Scripture and indicates a quick, sudden aggressive snatching. The place of meeting is interesting. It is the realm of where the Devil had his 'seat' (Ephesians 2:2). The Lord of Glory is hereby making a statement. He is sovereign and in control. It should also be a 'wake-up' call to those left behind. The result of being caught up means we are forever with the Lord. Can you wonder why the apostle summons his readers, on the basis of this teaching, to encourage each other! They were having a tough time because of their commitment to Jesus and they were to stand firm and look beyond the immediate to the promise.

Paul continues to further explain the difference between the Church being seized up to the clouds and 'the day of the Lord'. This is an Old Testament term used often and it concentrates on Israel and the Nations. It is a devastating time affecting all the World. It is a day of wrath! Notice, however, what he writes to the Thessalonians. 'God has destined us (the Body of Christ, the Church) not for wrath but for obtaining salvation through our Lord Jesus Christ … Therefore encourage one another and build up each other, as indeed you are doing' (1 Thessalonians 5:9,11).

Until the loud command, the archangel's call and the trumpet sound …

Maranatha!

As a Thief He comes
Day 3

Verse: 'Know this: if the owner of the house had known at what hour the thief was coming, he would not have let his house be broken into. You also must be ready, for the Son of Man is coming at an unexpected hour,' Luke 12:39-40.

Six times the return of Jesus Christ to Earth is likened to a thief in the night. We will look briefly into four. A thief comes to steal and plunder. Jesus is coming to reclaim and to conquer. Although specific for the time of the great tribulation each reference has a special emphasis applicable to any period of time. What is written is both a warning and an encouragement to followers of Jesus. It is through their being on the lookout for Him that the world of the godless is also warned.

Luke's account surrounds the events of the master returning from his wedding banquet. According to the custom of the time there wasn't any certainty as to when the groom would go and claim his bride. Nor was there any timescale for his returning with her to the place he had prepared for them. The household slaves were expected to faithfully perform their work and keep a lamp burning whilst he was away. Jesus used the story to encourage His disciples to faithfulness even in doing their mundane chores. The amazing promise of the Master is that he will actually wait upon such a servant. What an incentive to be watchful.

Matthew uses the term in the context of Christ's teaching on the end times in chapter 24. Again it is to the Twelve. Through them we are informed about the blessing of faith with faithfulness and the curse of unbelief expressed in abuse. The unbelieving house manager imagined the Lord either delays returning or it is simply a myth. This unbelief unleashed abusive behaviour towards others unworthy of a disciple. 'The master of that slave will come on a day when he does not expect him and at an hour that he does not know' (Matthew 24:30). The result is judgement, dismissal and eternal sorrow.

John offers consolation to those facing tribulation. This is dealing with the final and terrible tribulation to come. However, it also encompasses Christ's servants enduring similar experiences across the centuries. Within the context of Revelation the scenario is the countdown to Armageddon. Believers in Christ are having a rugged time and the Lord inserts a blessing. 'See, I am coming like a thief! Blessed is the one who stays awake and is clothed, not going about naked and exposed to shame.' (Revelation 16:15).

Persecution aims to make a believer recant their faith or die. Christ's opponents want to rob the believers of their promised reward and have them appear naked in God's sight. The clothing they seek to strip away is the righteousness of Christ. Believers are marked out because of their godly behaviour in a depraved and violent society. The Lord Christ says to them, indeed to all of us, 'remain faithful, the blessing is more than the pain.' One is for a short time but the other is eternal, The Lord revealed the end of the story to empower His people to endure.

Peter tells us 'The day of the Lord will come like a thief, and then the heavens will pass away with a loud noise, and the elements will be dissolved with fire, and the earth and everything that is done on it will be disclosed' (2 Peter 3:10). This aspect of the Lord's return ushers in the longed for New Heavens and New Earth. Again we ask 'why was this written?' Answer: Since all these things are to be dissolved in this way, what sort of followers ought you to be in leading lives of holiness and godliness? (verse 11).

The thief in the night is Jesus' way to keep us 'on our toes'. He knows we will be subjected to scoffing, abuse and the temptation to doubt. Along with the call to be alert the Lord also supplied resources to sustain. We are not left to our own devices. Jesus has provided His Holy Spirit, His Word and His Church. Thank you lord!

Maranatha!

Why God Laughs
Day 4

Verse: 'He who sits in the heavens laughs; the Lord holds them in derision... "I have set my king on Zion, my holy hill"' Psalm 2:4-6

God is no stoic, free from passion and unmoved by events on earth. He shares in the experiences of His people as Isaiah 63:9 records, 'In all their affliction he was afflicted ...'(KJV). This is also pictured by Christ's words to Saul on the road to Damascus. "Saul, Saul, why do you persecute me?" (Acts 9:4). Our Lord feels the pain when His people are afflicted and will not remain indifferent to their suffering. The Biblical record shows us numerous times when Yahweh intervened for the sake of His covenant people. It should not surprise us, therefore, when we read Psalm 2 and read about the Lord showing His emotions. This psalm also outlines the sadness behind why God laughs and the consequences which follow. It is the claim of both Testaments that God is King of kings and Lord of lords. This annoys Lucifer the usurper who has constantly attempted to dethrone the Creator and Redeemer.

What began under Nimrod in Genesis 10:8 has been a relentless endeavour ever since. He is marked as the first in a long list of opponents to the rule of God who act in defiance of His commands. This psalm is prophetic as it points to the future culmination of the 'Nimrod' rebellion. Under the influence of Satan an earthly international conspiracy is formed. Notice key words in the first three verses. These nations, conspire, plot, take counsel and want to burst the bonds and cast off the cords. All of this is because the nations refuse to have Yahweh's anointed rule over them. What are they trying to smash and throw away? It doesn't say. It would be fair to assume the people wanted to do their own thing, live without the Lord's commands and the 'yoke' of His righteousness. The objective of the nations' military thrust is to cause God's word to fail. When you read the prophets such as Joel, it is clear where all this plotting leads: A military campaign. It's designed to destroy Israel and the rule of Christ. Their intention is to install the ultimate expression of Nimrod in the Jerusalem temple. Unbelief and hatred combine to make individuals and nations blind, deaf and unbalanced toward history, Scripture and the sheer folly of their actions.

God's scornful laughter is actually the grief of grace. He has recorded His intentions. He has offered mercy to all who would kiss the feet of His anointed. He has warned the rulers of nations of the danger of their actions. Yahweh's offer however, is only available until the nations implement their intentions. Then grace becomes wrath unlimited. Their intentions to dethrone the Christ and trample His commands rebounds upon their own 'heads.' The Biblical principle, you reap what you sow, is once again demonstrated.

The picture of God 'sitting' presents us with the reality of Him being in control. In His mind the King on Zion's hill is an accomplished fact (read days 19, 25). All the furious activity is from the human side of the battle. The groundwork for this confrontation has been building up for a long time. Today's world is no different. Apostasy within Christendom gives support to the scoffers who say, 'Where is the promise of His coming? For ever since our ancestors died, all things continue as they were from the beginning of creation' (2 Peter 3:4). This is a direct challenge to the Character of God and His word. It can only lead to the sad sound of Yahweh's laugh. Even so,

Maranatha!

The Dark City's Overthrow
Day 5.

Verse: 'Rejoice over her, O heaven, you saints and apostles and prophets! For God has given judgement for you against her' Revelation 18:20.

Two cities dominate the story of Scripture. Babylon is mentioned first as it appears after the worldwide flood under Nimrod's influence. Jerusalem emerges later and becomes central to God's promise to Abraham. The spiritual power of these two cities are defined as Darkness and Light, Unrighteousness versus Righteousness, deceit against Truth. These two cities are on a collision course and only one can prevail. How did this state of affairs come about? By the arrogant pride of Lucifer. He had made Babylon his centre of operations to overthrow the Lord God Almighty (Isaiah 14:12-23). Part of his strategy was, and remains, the destruction of Israel and all who claim Jesus as the Messiah, the Son of the Living God.

The essence of the conflict centres on Babylon's claim '"I am", and there is no one besides me' (Isaiah 47:8). By that, Babylon is actually usurping the Lord God's revelation of His own name in Exodus 3:14. Here is a direct challenge to God's person and the commandment 'You shall have no other gods before me.' What this city did was a declaration of war. There can only be one Sovereign. There can only be one before whom all creation bows. The Bible has a lot to say about Babylon from a historical and a prophetic viewpoint. Though beaten by the Medes and Persians as an empire its spirit and hatred towards God continues. Babylon is foretold to arise as a city from the rubble of history and reign in the Great Tribulation period. Revelation points to the time of its evil resurgence under the Anti-Christ.

Babylon is shown to become the source of wealth for the elite, the haunt of demons and the courtesan of the World rulers. She is the centre of sorcery and the slave trade; her 'hands' are covered in the blood of Christ's prophets and saints. This city gives the appearance of a good time without any moral boundaries as she rules as a queen (Revelation 18). Why then hasn't Christ stepped in and obliterated Babylon long ago? Psalm 75:7-8 provides an insight. 'It is God who executes judgement, putting down one and lifting up another. For in the hand of the Lord there is a cup with foaming wine, well mixed; he will pour a draught from it, and all the wicked of the earth shall drain it down to the dregs.' When the cup of wrath is full and not before, God makes the Dark City drink.

Another reason is found in His desire to offer all under the spell of Babylon an escape route to a new destiny. Jesus offers this hope of a new beginning before He takes action to pour out His wrath on those who remain in Babylon. His offer is, 'Come out of her my people, so that you do not take part in her sins…' (Revelation 18:4). How can people come out of a moral and spiritual realm which is so persuasive, so powerful and so pleasing to the sinful nature? Not by religious rituals, distinctive garments, good intentions or better morals! The answer can only be found in the Person who has breached the enemy's defences, discredited and triumphed over its claims and power. That is the message of the cross! Colossians 1:13-14, 'He has rescued us from the power of darkness and transferred us into the kingdom of his beloved Son, in whom we have redemption, the forgiveness of sins.' Coming out results in a moral and spiritual transformation achieved by a change of allegiance.

When the 'cup is full' and the promised return of Jesus as the warrior Lord is about to happen then Babylon's judgement occurs. It happens quickly. Then Heaven erupts into singing "Hallelujah!" Followed by the twenty-four elders and the four living creatures saying, "Amen. Hallelujah!" These are in turn followed by the voice of a great multitude in unison crying out, "Hallelujah!" Why? The Lord God of Heaven, His word and justice have been vindicated (Revelation 19).

Maranatha!

The Day of God's Jealousy
Day 6

Verse: 'The Lord became jealous for his land, and had pity on his people' Joel 2:18.

God, Jealous! The mind recoils in horror. Our sense of jealousy places it in the sin basket. How then can we reconcile 'you shall worship no other god, because the Lord, whose name is Jealous, is a jealous God' (Exodus 20:5, 34:14)?

Our Lord, the Creator, can be jealous of no–one and no–thing. He is however Jealous on behalf of [1]His name, [2]His people, [3]His city and His land. Those who defile one aspect actually despise all. The result is that the Lord's jealousy becomes zealousness as He defends that which He holds precious. There is an example of this in the life of Jesus. He never tried to defend Himself, He did however express His passion in defending His Father's name. When Jesus saw the abuse taking place in the temple He made a whip and chased the sellers out. He upturned their tables and the disciples recalled Psalm 69:9, 'Zeal for your house will consume me.' Whilst the incident is related to the physical act in the temple it has a far wider message. According to 1 Timothy 3:15 believers in Jesus as the risen Lord and Saviour are called 'The Household of God.' The implication is that those who defile 'God's Household' will be called to account.

Joel, as a sample of the prophets, welds jealous and zealous together in the 'Day of the Lord.' The prophets used this specific term and refer it to God's intervention into the affairs of the nations. It is a judging time graphically described in Nahum chapter 1. Across Biblical and general histories you can discern God calling specific nations to account. His dealings with His apostate nation of Israel are also recorded. They are disciplined but not cast off, sidelined but not destroyed. Then there is the scenario of the Gentile kingdoms featured in Daniel 2. Three of the four mentioned have been judged. The fourth kingdom has yet to fill its cup of iniquity. When the 'cup' overflows the Day of the Lord comes (Joel 2:31).

How is God's jealousy aroused? The prophets foresaw the [4]land God calls his own being defiled and ravaged. The United Nations promotes the myth that Israel never had any ancient association with 'the Promised land.' Israel as God's people have been historically, and are seen prophetically as, exploited, expelled and many exterminated. The Gentile nations were meant to be the Lord's scourge, not executioner, of Israel. To go beyond His purpose to refine and awaken His people aroused the ire of the Lord. Joel's summing up of the end time events could well be, "Enough! Times up!" Full and overflowing will be the cup of God's judgement and wrath the Nations will be made to drink on that day. Where will this take place? In the [5]valley of decision! In that valley God tells us "Therefore wait for me, says the Lord, for the day when I arise as a witness. For my decision is to gather nations, to assemble kingdoms, to pour out upon them my indignation, all the heat of my anger; for in the fire of my passion (jealousy) all the earth shall be consumed" (Zephaniah 3:8).

When 'the Lord roars from Zion, and utters his voice from Jerusalem, and the heavens and the earth shake. ... the Lord [will be] a refuge for his people, a stronghold for the people of Israel' (Joel 3:16). God never abandons those He calls His own. This doesn't mean they are immune from going through hard times. It does mean He is their security, their hope, their refuge and their companion in their affliction. God's jealous zeal may seem to take a long time to be aroused. He understands that but calls upon us to wait, trust and be faithful. He sees the total picture. He acts with holy zeal. He honours His word! His justice will be delivered!

Maranatha!

[1]Deuteronomy 4:23-24. Ezekiel 39:25. [2] Ezekiel 36:5-7. [3]Zechariah 1:14, 8:2.

[4]Leviticus 25:23. Deuteronomy 11:12. [5] Joel 3:14

Back in Residence
Day 7

Verse: 'The glory of the God of Israel was coming from the east…the glory of the Lord entered the temple by the gate facing east' Ezekiel 43:2-4.

Solomon built a temple to honour the Lord God, creator of the Universe. He, who all creation cannot contain, made Himself known there by the cloud of His presence (2 Chronicles 7:1). Whilst the Lord's presence remained the city was safe. However, Yahweh had warned that unrepentant rebellion to His Law would result in His leaving the temple. This would leave the city vulnerable to being completely overthrown by hostile forces. For the Lord was their defence and shield, not the swords or the horses of Israel or its alliances.

History records the fulfilment of this warning. It happened under Nebuchadnezzar. What isn't so readily realised is the heartbreak of God. The action of God leaving the temple of His beloved city is simply and poignantly recorded in several verses in the book of Ezekiel. Between chapters 8 and 11 the reader can discern God's reluctant retreat. Ezekiel 11:27 'The glory of the Lord ascended from the middle of the city, and stopped on the mountain east of the city.' That mountain is the Mount of Olives! The last mention of the presence of God in relation to His presence in Jerusalem is here. What is the significance of this connection with 'the glory' and the mountain? Scripture leads us to the answer!

Another Temple was commenced when the Jewish people returned from Babylonian captivity. Zerubbabel was the leader in this undertaking. We know that the Temple was adorned centuries later by King Herod. Here the Lord Jesus worshipped, taught and cast out the corrupt marketeers. The Son of God claimed that the temple was meant to be the Father's house and a place of prayer. This magnificent building with its impressive ritual was missing the presence of Yahweh. He had not returned! As such it can be seen as an illustration of those who have a form of godliness but do not have the presence of the Lord.

This temple was destroyed by the Romans in A.D.70. Will another be built? Looking at today's political landscape most would say "Impossible"! Islamic opposition and United Nations' rejection of Israel's right to the mount would support that 'Impossible'! Here is in fact a direct challenge to the Lord God's word and integrity. He has already revealed the future. Jesus, in talking of the End Times, spoke of a temple on the same site. In Ezekiel chapters 40-48 are found elaborate details of the promised temple.

When Jesus came to Bethlehem it was as the Warrior Baby. He fought the fight for our redemption and the rule of God on the cross. What appeared to be His defeat became His glorious victory. Forty days later He too went to the Mount of Olives. From there He ascended to His Father's presence. A promise was made there and then that 'this same Jesus' would return visibly, on the clouds and to that same mount (Acts 1:9-11). Zechariah the prophet foresaw this return. 'Then the Lord will go forth and fight against those nations as when he fights on a day of battle. On that day his feet shall stand on the mount of Olives, which lies between Jerusalem on the east.' (Zechariah 14:3-4) Can you see the link with Ezekiel, Acts 1 and Zechariah? Do you grasp the meaning and intent? The One who left the temple, the one who was crucified, the one who rose from the tomb, the one who ascended is the one who returns to the Mount of Olives. He is 'the glory.' He is the Lord. His name is Jesus the Christ, the Son of God!

After the Lord conquers the forces against Him the prophet Ezekiel saw the following: 'Then he brought me to the gate, the gate [of the temple] facing east. And there, the glory of the God of Israel was coming from the east [the Mount of Olives]; the sound was like the sound of mighty waters and the earth shone with the glory' (Ezekiel 43:2). The Lord God of Hosts was returning to where He promised to make His presence known forever. It will be to this temple that individuals and nations will come and celebrate the victory He gained. The Warrior Lord will then be able to put aside the sword and take up the sceptre of peace. From this place and by His presence the righteous Law and the power of Grace will flow [Isaiah 2.] Praise the Lord!

Maranatha!

Reflection/Study#1.

*What moments in your life do you really long for the return of the Lord and cry out 'Maranatha!?

*From the various references to Jesus coming as a 'Thief in the night' what impressed you the most?

*Share your insights about the emotions of God.

*Babylon was condemned for usurping the description 'I AM'. As Jesus used this on a number of occasions what is it revealing about Him?

*How do you respond to the jealousy of God?

*Personal insights from the devotionals 1-7.

Maranatha!

Preparing for the Return.
Day 8

Verse: 'In my father's house there are many dwelling places. If it were not so, would I have told you that I go to prepare a place for you? And if I go and prepare a place for you I will come again and take you to myself' John 14:2-3.

It had been an exhausting week. The countdown to the cross was well underway and still Jesus taught, debated and made arrangements for the Passover. He must have been exhausted. The account in John 13 – 17 contains His final words to the eleven. In chapter 14 we catch a glimpse of Jesus in a special light. At Bethlehem we encounter His entry into humanity on our behalf. At the cross we grasp the depth of His mission. Here, in the upper room, in this intimate setting the deity of Jesus once more is revealed.

In my Father's house there are many dwelling places

Calling God His Father raised the ire of the people. They were ready to stone Him (John 10:33). I doubt the disciples really grasped the significance even now. They trusted Jesus and for the moment that was enough. It was Thomas, after the resurrection, who framed those beautiful words of faith 'my Lord and my God' (John 20:28).

When He used the term 'my Father's house' was Jesus thinking of any specific place? In this gospel the term is used fourteen times. Essentially it is undefined. Where the Lord God is, there is His house. Rest assured, there is plenty of room for us to have our own space (if we ever needed it). Perhaps the last mention of God's abode gives us a clue to our future destiny. Revelation 21:1-4 calls it the Heavenly Jerusalem.

I go to prepare a place for you

Why was it necessary for a place in the Father's realm to be prepared? 'It was necessary for the sketches of the heavenly things to be purified by these [earthly] rites, but the heavenly things themselves need better sacrifices than these' (Hebrews 9:23). We know Christ's shed blood purified the realm contaminated by Satan's rebellion and Adam's sin. The way Jesus had to go to achieve all this was the cross. The New Jerusalem cannot abide in an unclean universe.

Therefore for anyone to join Jesus they must have had a similar cleansing. Paul's word to Titus tells us, 'we wait for the blessed hope and the manifestation of the glory of our great God and Saviour Jesus Christ. He it is who gave himself for us that he might redeem us from all iniquity and purify for himself a people of his own who are zealous for good deeds' (Titus 2:13-14). The place is probably prepared by now. Why then does He wait? God's purposes and His designated time are the answer!

I will come again and take you to myself.

In most other references to the second coming it mentions the 'Son of Man.' Here Jesus identifies Himself un–mistakably as that prophesied person. Grasp the strength in the '*I will come again*!' It is an unbreakable promise. Jesus didn't endure the cross simply to melt away into the mists of history. The Risen Lord will return to complete the mission. He will honour His word. The strength also in the words of '*take you to myself*' lays in the fact that no one, nor anything can prevent it.

For what purpose? '*So that where I am, there you may be also.*'

The discourse of John 17:20, 24 amplifies this wonderfully: 'I ask not only on behalf of these (the eleven) but also on behalf of those who will believe in me through their word…Father, I desire that those also, whom, you have given me, may be with me where I am, to see my glory, which you have given me because you loved me before the foundation of the world.' Imagine that. Jesus desires our company with Him in His Father's house for ever. By faith Jesus shares our life now. Then, we shall see Him in all His glory. What an awesome destiny Jesus has given us.

Maranatha!

As in the Day of Noah
Day 9

Reading: 'For as the days of Noah were, so will be the coming of the Son of Man' Matthew 24:37.

It is the most important boat in history. The ark was made to be a refuge from the judgement of the worldwide flood, God's judgement on unmitigated evil. In it He preserved four men and four women plus animals and other earth bound creatures. Genesis 6 – 9 records it was a time of corruption, violence, demonic activity and minds set only on evil. Jesus described the time of Noah, 'In those days before the flood they were eating and drinking, marrying and giving in marriage… until the flood came' (Matthew 24:37-39). The term 'eating and drinking' is very revealing when compared to other passages where the term is used. Exodus 32 is the account of the Golden Calf idolatry when, 'they [people of Israel] rose early the next day and brought sacrifices of well-being; and the people sat down to eat and drink, and rose up to revel.' Idolatry is the hand–maiden to sexual immorality, demonic activity and associated evils (1 Corinthians 10:5-8. Daniel 5:1f).

From the brief account in Genesis it is easy for folk to presume God to be callous, even cruel in destroying that civilization through water. Those of us who know the Lord and His word appreciate the fact that He is holy and gracious, just and merciful. How does that come out in this setting? The people had the choice of believing or rejecting the ways of Yahweh. Too often we hear 'seeing is believing' which doesn't work out in practise. Adam and Eve lived for 930 years after their expulsion from Eden. Many people would have known Adam's story either first or second hand. Their story would have borne testimony to Yahweh's holiness and justice. Also, the Garden of Eden was still in existence and could have been seen from the outside. Remember, it was guarded by the Cherubim with drawn swords. Enoch's being taken up into God's presence surely would have been newsworthy (Genesis 5). Then there is Noah's work of building the ark. He is called a herald of righteousness in 2 Peter 2:5. Not one of those who perished could accuse God of being unfair, unjust or impatient. Similar words will apply to people at the return of Christ.

Noah was God's last word to and about that era. How did he find grace in the sight of the Lord? Hebrews 11:6-7: 'By faith Noah, warned by God about events as yet unseen, respected the warning and built an ark ...'. The testimony of godly forerunners would have made Noah aware of and sensitive to hearing God's voice. Their stories about God's dealings would have been passed down from family to family. As with us, so with them, the critical issue was a faith founded on fact which motivated a person to commitment. We too are to bear witness to our generation and to teach the next generation God's story. Noah was prepared to stand up and stand out from the unbelief of his day. He wore their mocking in building the boat in the confidence that he would be ultimately vindicated.

Jesus linked His return to the time of Noah to show us the World is not on a self–improvement course. Without the ministry of God's Word and the transforming power of the Cross the World merely degenerates. Every age and every society is infected with the self–destructiveness of unbelief, idolatry and rebelliousness. This will culminate in the judgement of God spoken of 'as in the days of Noah.' God in grace provided a safe place in Noah's day so He has provided one at the end times. The Name of that refuge is Christ Jesus! Faith is the 'passport' which provides entrance into the safe place. In what or who is this faith placed? It is Jesus as the Lord and Saviour crucified, entombed and risen from the dead who delivers us from this evil world and the coming wrath.

Maranatha!

Being Confident when He Comes
Day 10

Verse: 'Now little children abide in him, so that when he is revealed we may have confidence and not be put to shame before him at his coming' 1 John 2:28.

'Grand-father' John, the apostle, reveals his heart when writing to the Church. He calls the readers his 'children' and desires the best for them. John had issued a warning about those who misrepresent or disparage Jesus the Christ. He offered the readers their best protection against such opposition, 'now, little children, abide in him.' In other words, remain calm, know and enjoy the strength of your faith relationship.

Abide is a favourite word of John. It is a warm word which expresses a sense of security in and with Jesus Christ. What he wrote then still applies. 1 John 2:6, whoever says, "I abide in him," ought to walk as he walked.' The apostle uses this word to lead the reader from abiding by knowledge into abiding through fellowship. This relationship is expressed by consistency of devotion to Christ, not faultlessness.

To abide in Christ also produces an inner assurance and hope towards a future event. This is behind the word 'So that when he is revealed we may have confidence ...' According to Vincent's Word Studies confidence has the idea of 'free, open speech... coming before God's bar with nothing to conceal.' There is the sense of boldness, not arrogance, woven into it. This boldness does not come from personal worth but from the embracing grace of Christ Jesus.

Such confidence means we are looking forward to meeting Him who is the source and object of our faith. It vibrates with an expectation that He will be pleased to accept us. How different it will be for those who may be ashamed to stand before Jesus the Lord when He comes again. What would cause any of us to be ashamed of meeting the Lord? In a word, unbelief. This spiritual virus can infect any of us and will make its presence known.

How? By watering down or disobeying His commands, neglect of worship and stewardship, unrighteousness and faithlessness to highlight only five.

A disciple may, in this life, cover such infections by many and varied strategies. However, on the day when the Lord appears such 'covers' dissolve. Those disciples will find themselves naked. The word 'before Him' can also be translated 'from him.' The word picture is of the individual who wants to shrink, hide or run from the all revealing presence of the Lord. How sad! Jesus will not have to say a word. His presence is enough to make the person quake with shame.

But there is an antidote for unbelief: 2 Timothy 1:12, 'I am not ashamed, for I know the one in whom I have put my trust, and am sure that he is able to guard until that day what I have entrusted to him.' Knowing Christ Jesus in an ongoing faith relationship counteracts unbelief. Knowing leads to gratitude. Gratitude stimulates confidence. Confidence motivates obedience. Obedience enriches faith. The beauty and promise of all this is tasted in the word 'abiding' when it is linked to 'in Him'.

John stressed a future point in time in the two words 'revealed' and 'coming.' Revealed is to make manifest what has been hidden. It is a different word to revelation (apocalypse) which will be considered later. When Jesus reveals Himself we will be drawn into a deeper appreciation of who He is. Jesus the crucified, captivates our focus on earth, on the occasion John writes about we will behold Jesus the Lord of glory. When will all this happen? 'At his coming!' That is the time when His presence is visible and every eye will see Him (Matthew 24:30). Many will quake in terror. Others will shudder with embarrassment. For 'abiding' believers, there will be great rejoicing.

Maranatha!

The Three in One Shepherd
Day 11

Verse: 'The Lord is my shepherd, I shall not want' Psalm 23:1.

God is the Master mathematician and He enjoys using specific numbers. Within His word they play an important and consistent role with spiritual significance. Numbers which quickly spring to mind are, 1, 3, 7, 8, and 10 although there are others. The number three we will consider as it relates to a title of Jesus. Three (3) points to completeness, to that which is entire within itself and real. In the New Testament there are three references to Jesus in His role as shepherd. Each one builds on the other, two without the third would present an incomplete picture.

Christians know and love the description of the Lord as the Good Shepherd in John 10. He made a contrast between a shepherd and a hireling. One flees danger. The shepherd however gives his life for the sheep. When He designated Himself 'the good Shepherd' there is an implied reference to His Deity. From the young ruler's words to Jesus in Luke 18:18, "good teacher..." and the Lord's reply, "No one is good but God alone"! Jesus didn't deny the words and let them rest as seeds for a future springing forth of their truthfulness. Jesus is Emmanuel, God with us, which became apparent after the events of Calvary. There it was as the smitten Shepherd He surrendered His life to save His creation. It is also worthy of note that three languages, Greek, Latin, and Hebrew were nailed above His head. This symbolises the completeness of the World's rejection of Jesus.

The second description of Jesus is in Hebrews 13:20: 'Now may the God of peace who brought back from the dead our Lord Jesus, the great shepherd of the sheep, by the blood of the eternal covenant.' Why is He great? Because of the resurrection! He conquered the forces intent upon the eternal destruction of the flock. All that Psalm 22 foretold, and the Gospels record about His enemies and His death, Jesus faced, suffered and overcame. There is none greater. He is pre-eminent in all of history and eternity. Now the Psalm most dear to our hearts can be activated. Psalm 23 is the resurrection promise.

The third and final revelation about Jesus in this capacity is from 1 Peter 5:4: 'When the chief shepherd appears, you will win the crown of glory that never fades away.' Without this assurance the work of the Lord Jesus would be incomplete. What use would be the crucifixion without a resurrection? What purpose the resurrection without Jesus returning to rule and lead His 'flock'? Peter used the term as an example to and a motivation especially for the leaders of the church community. It will be at Christ's coming again that we will behold His true glory. For His people it will be a delight. For those who still seek to deny Him and His reign and to destroy His followers there will be disaster.

What Psalm would you place alongside this wonderful completion of the role of Jesus Christ as Shepherd? Psalm 24! It is the song of the returning shepherd King. This expressive term for the Kings of Israel was given because of David. When he was called to the throne he had been a shepherd. The unfortunate sadness of so many of his descendents was that they didn't have a shepherd's heart. They were more like the hirelings who tore and mauled God's people. Jesus Christ of the human line of David came to live out what it means to be the Good, the Great and the Chief Shepherd.

As the Good Shepherd, Jesus redeemed us. As the Great Shepherd, He rose to secure that salvation. At this moment Jesus is exercising His role as our Shepherd intercessor in His heavenly realm (Hebrews 7:25). Sometime during that role Christ Jesus will put aside His intercession to gird on His battledress. Then He will return to earth and fulfil the position as our Chief Shepherd. Psalm 24 would seem fitting to be sung on that day. 'Lift up your heads, O gates! And be lifted up, O ancient doors! That the King of glory may come in. Who is the King of glory? The Lord, strong and mighty, the Lord mighty in battle.'

Maranatha!

Heaven's Hallelujah Chorus
Day 12

Verse: 'Hallelujah!" Salvation and glory and power to our God, for His judgments are true and just' Revelation 19:1.

Singing is mentioned more in Revelation than any other New Testament book. It resounds with the music of salvation, testimony and justice. Too often people are so pre-occupied by debating aspects of the book that they miss its music. Revelation was written to bless us. It was also to get our hearts to feel the excitement and the wonder of the Christ whose name we wear. It was to prepare His people to join one of the choirs in the sky. For in this book there are six distinct references to groups singing and worshipping the almighty and Holy God.

Revelation 11 introduces the elders with the four living creatures and their song. There they are rejoicing over the Lord God Almighty who is exercising His sovereign right to reign. When the saints burst into song the elders and living creatures are similar to a backing group. "Amen. Hallelujah!" is their harmonising agreement (Revelation 19:4). Time was up! Accounting time had come. God's patience had ended. Now it is time for the Lord to reward His servants. Now is the time for the Lord of heaven's Hosts to end earth's anarchy.

The choir in Revelation 19 is immense. Their song is the climax of the chapters preceding it. Now the overthrow of and judgment upon Babylon is celebrated. This city which had corrupted the world with her sorceries had just been destroyed by a single stroke from the Lord. The harlot city's demise produced a rapturous response of praise in the Heavens. "Hallelujah" burst from the lips of a great multitude. They sang of salvation and justice secured by the Lamb in verses 1-2. This was a far different song from Revelation 4 where the living creatures and the elders sang to the Creator. In chapter 5 these two groups sang about redemption through the blood of the Lamb. Now a new choir of the saints rejoices in the destruction of the 'woman sitting on a scarlet beast … "Babylon the great" … drunk with the blood of the saints.' Prayers, held by God over time as mentioned in Revelation 6:9-11, were now answered.

In Revelation 19:5 a voice from the throne invites the choir of the great multitude to praise God once more. The response is overwhelming. The sound is as many waters and mighty thunderpeals. What a glorious sound the apostle would have heard. He must have tingled all over at its reverberation and passion. "Hallelujah" shatters the universe as the choral group brings their song to its crescendo. Some may feel a little uncomfortable about celebrating God's vengeance in song. Read the Scriptures about the depravity, degradation and dealing in death by this satanic city. Surely that will change their view. God's judgment is just because it comes from His holiness as His patience reaches its limit.

This song is the declaration that the Lord our God the Almighty reigns. What was a statement of faith is now the song of reality. 'Let us rejoice and exult and give him the glory.' Constantly the desire to bear testimony to the glory and wonder of God permeates this book. What was the reason for the excitement of the multitude? Now the marriage of the Lamb could take place. The bride He had died for, the bride He rose for and made beautiful, the bride of Ephesians 5:25-27 was now ready. The marriage supper was ready. Then we read about the Lord God of Hosts going off to complete the final judgment on the Anti–Christ and false prophets. As He rode to the battle there would be fire in His eyes and the Hallelujah chorus ringing in His heart.

Maranatha!

A Forgotten Reason
Day 13

Verse:' When he comes to be glorified by his saints and to be marvelled at on that day among all who have believed...' 2 Thessalonians 1:10.

This second letter by Paul to the Thessalonians takes us beyond those believers into a future time. These disciples become representatives of those who accept Christ as Lord across centuries. History records there is a price to be paid for joining Christ's company. Paul's words of encouragement and the promise of justice when the Saviour returns is designed to empower them, and us, to endure. The humiliation of the Church of Christ by a hostile society reflects the experience of Jesus and what he suffered at the cross. However, by the power His resurrection, humiliation gave way to glory.

As second Thessalonians unfolds it is this glory which shines through. There is the glory of proving God's choice of the believer as being worthy of the Kingdom (1:5). There is the glory that in and through the disciple's faithfulness the name of Jesus is glorified (1:12). There is the glory for the Thessalonians as the first fruits of the Gospel in their region. They, along with others, share in the glory of the Lord Jesus Christ (2:13-14). It is this glory Jesus talked about with His Father in John 17. The Lord wanted His people to behold and share in His glory. The narrow way into that majestic realm is opened by the Gospel. Handling humiliation and persecution is part of the cross we take up in a Christ rejecting society.

On the day of His return this letter records the reaction of the Christians: they marvel at Him. The word can also be translated as 'admire'. The pent-up emotion caused by the dramatic yet tragic events prior to the return burst apart in praise and admiration. He whom they have believed in by faith is now seen. He whom they have served is before them. He whom they have loved without seeing is now amongst them as the conqueror. To picture this moment is nigh on impossible. To see Him in His battle garment, His righteousness radiating its brilliance, will be awesome, in the truest sense of the word. To have witnessed His triumph with the sword of His mouth, the breath of judgment, will leave all speechless: awestruck. That is, until there surges forth from countless lips praise to the Lord, King of kings. What was sung on the day He entered Jerusalem on the donkey, and not really believed by the masses, now comes true. "Hosanna to the Son of David! Blessed is the one who comes in the name of the Lord! Hosanna in the highest heaven!"

Is it at this moment I John 3:2 is experienced? We cannot say. However, it is possible! 'What we know is this: when he is revealed, we will be like him, for we will see him as he is.' Here is a longing within the heart. Job may be the first to record it when he wrote, 'I know my Redeemer lives, and that at the last he will stand upon the earth; and after my skin has been destroyed, then in my flesh I shall see God' (Job 19:25-26). David in Psalm 17 has a similar longing; 'as for me, I shall behold your face in righteousness; when I awake I shall be satisfied, beholding your likeness.' All this leads us to a wonderful fulfilment of their longing, in Philippians 3:20-21. 'Our citizenship is in heaven, and it is from there that we are expecting a Saviour, the Lord Jesus Christ. He will transform the body of our humiliation that it may be conformed to the body of his glory, by the power that also enables him to make all things subject to himself.'

This Thessalonian letter is a call for Christ's followers to turn the negative of affliction, humiliation and loss into a testimony. Whatever our views of the Lord's return this truth remains unscathed, we shall behold Him! We shall be transformed in the twinkling of an eye. We shall be like Him! Let us live out, sound out and rejoice about this truth.

Maranatha!

The Dream, the Idol and the Stone
Day 14

Verse: 'The stone that struck the statue became a great mountain and filled the whole earth' Daniel 2: 35.

Dreams play an interesting role within Scripture. The first dream came to Abimelech, King of Gerar (Genesis 20:3). Under the impression that Sarah was Abraham's sister, he took her into his harem. By this dream God protected not only Sarah and Abraham but also the King. Dreams also came to [1]Joseph, [2]Pharaoh, and the [3]Magi among many others. Nebuchadnezzar's dreams, recorded in Daniel, became God's opportunity to inform about coming events. Daniel, a young captive from Jerusalem selected for special training, became God's spokesman. 'There is a God in heaven who reveals mysteries, and has disclosed to King Nebuchadnezzar what will happen at the end of days' (Daniel 2:28). Four kingdoms were specifically mentioned. The head of gold is Babylon. Chest and arms of silver represent Medes and Persians. The middle and thighs are bronze are Greece, the legs of iron with feet mixed with iron and clay highlight Rome.

It is interesting to note that these kingdoms are represented by an idol, magnificent but decaying. An idol is always an abomination to the Lord God. He used this abomination to teach a number of future events and they all affect Israel. The significance of the head of gold representing Babylon is hard to ignore. Babylon and its occult religious system at that time dominated and permeated the whole world. With its anti-God and occult obsession it was, and remains, the life force of the nations. So, four world empires are pictured in this huge idol but they are not separate idols. A common bond holds the four kingdoms into a unit best described as Satan's anti-Christ spirit.

Nebuchadnezzar saw in his dream the idol's destruction by a huge stone. 'As you [the king] looked on, a stone was cut out, not by human hands, and it struck the statue on its feet of iron and clay and broke them to pieces'

(Daniel 2:34). Daniel didn't give a time frame. He just said it will take place in the fourth kingdom's reign. To gauge the meaning of the ten toes and other related matters required centuries to pass. The apostle John was given the honour of the unveiling. What he wrote in Revelation deals with this fourth kingdom. Amidst the literalism mixed with symbolism, we are drawn to the conclusion of Nebuchadnezzar's dream. The Stone from out of the Rock, uncut by Human hands, returns to history. Where had it been hiding? Why the delay? The dream made no mention of a time lapse (see day 2).

Nebuchadnezzar's dream had focused his attention on the Rock. A study of this *Crushing Stone* (Daniel 2:34-35) presents us with a 'shadow' of Christ Jesus. Before this end time event the word of God reveals Him with the following and related descriptions:[4] *The rejected stone,* [5]*The Smitten Stone,* [6]*The Living Stone,* [7] *Foundation Stone,* and [8]*the Cornerstone.* Jesus will finally be seen as the exalted and [9]*Radiant Stone.* He who put aside His glory to redeem Creation and Humankind is the same person who is the coming conqueror [remember Psalm 2]. He will be exalted in time and eternity. Any person who refuses to claim Him their Saviour and Lord finds Jesus to be a *Stumbling block and a Rock of offence.* The consequences are not pleasant (Matthew 21:44).

Moses linked the Rock with God. 'I will proclaim the name of the Lord; ascribe greatness to our God! The Rock, his work is perfect, and all his ways are just' (Deuteronomy 32:4). The Psalmist delighted in this title for the Eternal, 'The Lord is my Rock, my fortress, and my deliverer, my God, my Rock in whom I take refuge' (Psalm 18:2). Daniel's account encourages us to see the *crushing Stone* in the same light. It is a reference to Jesus! His return will bring to an end Satan's abominations and defiance of the Almighty. Babylon is obliterated. Jesus is the Rock which becomes the Mountain which will fill the whole world (Daniel 2:35).

Some years after the first dream Nebuchadnezzar had another. It became his personal encounter with the Lord. At the end of the experience he said, 'I blessed the Most High, and praised and honoured the one who lives forever. For his sovereignty is an everlasting sovereignty, and his kingdom endures from generation to generation.'

Maranatha!

[1] Genesis 20:3. [2] Genesis 41:7. [3] Matthew 2:12. [4] Psalm 118:22. [5] Numbers 20:8–11

[6] 1 Peter 2:4. [7] 1 Corinthians 3:11. [8] 1 Peter 2:6. [9] Revelation 4:2-3.

Reflection/study #2

*From the context of the time, what would impress you about Enoch? (day 9)

*The signs about 'the days of Noah' are always present. However, are they increasing?

*What other 'Hallelujah's' are there in Scripture? (day 12)

*How can we glorify Jesus Christ in our midst by faith today?

*Personal choices from the devotionals 8-14.

God Clear Purpose
Day: 15

Verse: 'Now write what you have seen, what is, and what will take place after this.' Revelation 1:19

The Knights of the Round Table are famous for such virtues as chivalry. However, it would seem that they believed honour to be the most important. When a knight felt his honour had been sullied he would throw down 'the gauntlet,' which was his warrior gloves. To pick up the glove meant the challenge was accepted. This principle can be applied to the spiritual realm. Heaven has thrown down 'the gauntlet' to the principalities and powers of this world and their ruler, the Devil. God is zealous for His honour. It has been besmirched through idolatry, immorality, heresy and religious vanity. His Creation polluted. His Son, crucified. His Word desecrated. His offer of grace and forgiveness scoffed at. The forces opposing Him probably didn't want to accept the challenge. God gives them no choice. On Patmos the apostle John was shown the consequences of the contest.

This had been preceded by other challenges to the Legions and supporters of Lucifer. Consider Moses before Pharaoh and the Egyptian nation. Moses informed the Egyptians about Yahweh's impending judgements. The gauntlet was thrown down. Egypt had enslaved the descendants of Abraham, Isaac and Jacob and wouldn't release them. On top of that, Pharaoh scoffed at God's command and challenge to set them free! Now there was no withdrawing from the contest. The ultimate purpose, 'The Egyptians shall know that I am the Lord.' Much later a similar scenario took place between David and Goliath who had defied God and His army. Goliath would be defeated 'So that all the earth may know that there is a God in Israel.'

Daniel recorded future events dealing with the Messiah's first and second comings. Daniel chapter 9:20-27 is the countdown to the mystery of the cross. It was to 'finish the transgression, to put an end to sin, and to atone for iniquity, to bring in everlasting righteousness.' All is assembled under the title of 'the seventy weeks', a term actually describing weeks of years. A strict timetable, with no room for error, is set. It has been worked out that 69 weeks culminated in the cross. When the Lord read from Psalm 118:24, 'this is the day that the Lord has made' it included the fulfilment of the 69th week. Here a number of prophesies about the cross, including the Passover's fulfilment and the 'rejected stone', reached their climax. One week is still to be accounted for. In it is the appearing of another prince who defies the Lord God of Hosts. This usurper sets up an abomination in the temple. He makes and breaks a covenant with Israel. He cancels the sacrifices and offerings of Israel. He sets out to destroy Jerusalem and the people. All this fills out the final seven years which Revelation highlights and explains.

The Eternal God has spelt out His plans for future events so that no one should claim ignorance when they happen. He has made plain that His final gauntlet will be cast down and the final contest begins. Our Lord and Saviour has given us His sure and certain word. Peter's confidence stems from personal experience: 'So we have the prophetic message more fully confirmed. You will do well to be attentive to this as a lamp shining in a dark place' (2 Peter 1:19). The meaning of the Greek word for 'confirmed' is firm, steadfast. We build our faith and our destiny on the Rock of the Triune God's integrity and faithfulness. Why would God bother to reveal His purposes? Isaiah 48:3-5 answers that. Yes, this was spoken to Israel and was about certain matters plainly meant for them. However the principle is unchanging. 'I know that you are obstinate, and your neck is an iron sinew and your forehead brass, I declared them to you from long ago, before they came to pass I announced them to you, so that you would not say, "My idol did them, my carved image commanded them."'

The prophetic word will not be undermined, torn down or lost. God has made a commitment and in the fullness of time, it will come to fruition. Christmas and Easter events must be seen as expressions of God's honour. Scripture and history reveal how the forces of evil and corruption tried to prevent them from being fulfilled. Such attempts failed as will their final endeavour. Ezekiel chapters 34-39 records what God has revealed about Israel and the Nations. Here the overarching, undergirding and all-embracing reason behind today's opening verse is explained: 'They shall know that I am the Lord.' The World will be without excuse. God's people will be warned, watching and waiting!

Maranatha:

Insights into the Thousand Year Reign
Day 16

Verse: 'Blessed and holy are those who share in the first resurrection. Over these the second death has no power, but they will be priests of God and of Christ, and they will reign with him a thousand years' Revelation 20:6.

War is catastrophic. Victory, bitter sweet. This is true even after the triumph of Christ Jesus over the forces of Satan and the Anti–Christ. When you assemble the various passages dealing with the seven years of tribulation it is a horrible time. Earthquakes, famine, warring armies, murder, celestial darkness and falling stars, vile behaviour and idolatry are a few of the prophetic details of this time. Imagine the countries in ruins and the damaged hearts and minds of the survivors?

Usually people dwell upon the glory of the Lord, the wonder of playing on an asp's nest or rolling with a lion (Isaiah 11). To be part of the first resurrection reads as an idyllic experience, and in many ways it will be. Don't forget that it will also be a time for ministry. The parables of the talents (Matthew 25:14-30) and the ten servants and ten pounds (Luke 19:11-27) promise work, not a picnic. We may question and want to intrude and ask *'What'*, *'When'*, *'Why'*, of this 1000 year reign. *'Why'* is answered by the promise of Jesus. Those faithful will be put in charge of many things and even a certain number of cities.

'What,' would be the purpose of being so rewarded? Could it be linked with the rebuilding and restoration imperatives of the thousand year reign of Christ? Ezekiel seems to sum up this time succinctly. 'Thus says the Lord God: On the day that I cleanse you from all your iniquities, I will cause the towns to be inhabited, and the waste places shall be rebuilt. The land that was desolate shall be tilled, instead of being the desolation that it was in the sight of all who passed by. And they will say, "This land that was desolate has become like the Garden of Eden; and the waste and desolate and ruined towns are now inhabited and fortified."' The prophet

was speaking about Israel of course. We may assume the principle applies across the devastated globe.

Included in this rebuilding program will be the New Temple described in Ezekiel 40-44. We may not understand it all. This we can grasp, it will be a glorious building because the Lord will make His presence known there. (Ezekiel 43:1, 8)

'When,' is tied in with the regathering of the scattered people to their homelands. This is especially detailed by Jeremiah and Ezekiel whose writings concentrate on Israel. 'Thus says the Lord God: When I gather the house of Israel from the peoples among whom they were scattered, and manifest my holiness in them in the sight of the nations, then they shall settle on their own soil that I gave to my servant Jacob' (Ezekiel 28:25). The magnitude of the task becomes apparent. Faithfulness to the Lord and His calling in this life will be rewarded in the millennium with oversight of such ventures. As priests we will be involved with worship. As co-regents (now that is awesome grace) we will represent Him across the world. As such we would be expected to see that our Lord's will and the needs of the people are met.

According to Zechariah 14 the nations of the world will be expected to go to Jerusalem and celebrate the Feast of Tabernacles. Details are not given, however, is it off the mark to think Christ's priests and co-regents would have a role to play? The one thousand year time frame is not one long picnic or an excuse for laziness. There will be righteousness and truth, peace and joy in abundance (Isaiah 61:11). There will also be the privilege of sharing the good news about the Lord Jesus with the surviving nations around the world (Isaiah 66:18-21).

Maranatha!

The Parousia of Christ
Day 17

Verse: 'May the God of Peace himself sanctify you entirely, and may your spirit and soul and body be kept sound and blameless at the coming (Parousia) of our Lord Jesus Christ' 1 Thessalonians 5:23.

On the Mount of Olives, away from the pilgrims on the Temple area, the twelve asked Jesus some questions. Earlier, they had been disturbed by a statement when Jesus said the Temple would be destroyed. Now Jesus went even further. Responding to their inquiries He spoke about the Parousia of the Son of Man. Included were also features dealing with the end of the age.

Parousia is the Greek word for the presence of a person. It also could point to his or her approaching arrival. This word became a technical description for the coming of an emperor or some other prominent person to the district. This meant the people were to be prepared for such an event. The Lord used 'parousia' to define His return to earth as the Son of Man. In Matthew 16:13-16 Jesus asked His disciples who was 'the Son of Man?' They shared various opinions before Jesus asked "who do you say I am?" By doing this He allied Himself to the vision of Daniel 9:13. This was a reference to the Son of Man coming to establish the Kingdom of God. Daniel, a Jewish prisoner of war had risen to prominence in Babylon. As an old man, greatly respected and favoured by God, he foretold the Son of Man's Parousia.

Alone with His twelve, Jesus explained some of the events which would happen when Daniel's prophesy was being fulfilled. It would be the climax of the Age. It would be the beginning of a new era. The Sun would be darkened, the stars would be in free fall, and the powers of heaven shaken. It would be a frightening time for the tribes of the earth, especially those who defied the Almighty. There would be a significant sign in the heavens which would indicate the Parousia of the Son of Man. His arrival is on chariots of clouds and in the company of angels. The tribes of the world will mourn but Christ's followers will take heart as they behold their Lord's arrival. When He returns it isn't in silence nor in secret.

The New Testament fills in more details of events leading up to Christ's Parousia. Among them are things explaining Jesus' words about the Tribulation and the ending of the 'Times of the Gentiles' (Luke 21:24). We also have further information about the Man of Lawlessness who sets up the idol in the future Temple (2 Thessalonians 2). There will be a rebellion against the Lord Jesus and His people. That which restrained the man of Lawlessness is removed. Heaven isn't sitting idly by during this time. From that realm judgements are poured upon the earth. These are graphically shown by symbols and performed by the angels in Revelation. Their intent is to bring repentance through the awareness of the approaching Parousia.

Parousia becomes a motivational word to lift the believer's moral and spiritual tone. In the opening verse for today we read of Paul's longing and prayer for the readers. He asks the Lord to set them apart, to sanctify them, in the midst of an evil society. He wants their total being to be 'kept sound' which has the underlying meaning of being preserved. Added to that is that they be blameless. Paul had already used the word 'blameless' in a written prayer: 'May the Lord ... so strengthen your hearts in holiness that you may be blameless before our God and Father at the coming of the Lord with all his saints' (1Thessalonians 3:13).Then and at the conclusion of his letter the term 'parousia' is the reason for their lifestyle, their endurance and their hope. Christ's Parousia drives a person to repentance. 'Blameless' doesn't mean bruise and scar free. It means we have been healed, forgiven and restored.

Maranatha!

The Apocalypse of Christ
Day 18

Verse: 'So that the genuineness of your faith ...may be found to result in praise and glory and honour when Jesus Christ is revealed' 1 Peter 1:7.

In the Gospels it is clear that most folk considered the promised Messiah in terms of the Lord of Hosts, a warrior. Jesus, however, was among them as the Christ, the Suffering Servant of Isaiah 53. Jesus tried to explain this to Peter and the others by raising the matter of His death. But at that time it was outside their ability to grasp it. The Son of God first had to be the Son of Man so as to be the Messiah who redeems. The Gospels present Jesus in His journey to the cross to become the Passover Lamb and the other sacrificial offerings.

After Christ's resurrection the New Testament writers honour Jesus in His servant's role. Acts opens with Christ's ascension and the preaching of the Cross and Jesus as the Christ. The message of grace and salvation began impacting various levels of society. Now the Holy Spirit confronted believers and unbelievers to the reality of who Jesus is! It was time to unveil the majesty of the crucified one. The writers show us Christ Jesus in royal robes, no longer wearing a servant's garment. Passage after passage in the New Testament letters try to do justice to the Lord's glory. John's attempt to describe Jesus in this way is awesome, frightening and captivating. Here is the meaning of the Revelation. In Greek the word is *'apocalypse'* and means an unveiling. Therefore the book of Revelation, the 'apocalypse' is the unveiling of the real nature and ultimate purpose of Jesus Christ. Unfortunately, the term apocalypse is more often thought of in the context of catastrophic warfare or natural disasters.

Revelation opens with John sending greetings and celebrating the wonder of Christ's saving grace. (1:5).Then in verse 6 the dramatic change the cross has made in believers is mentioned. We have been freed from our sins and made to be a kingdom, priests serving God. Verse 7 tells of the promise of the return of Christ Jesus but there is nothing new in any of that. Suddenly, there is a change in John's writing. Into his island prison steps the 'Alpha and the Omega, who is and who was and who is to come, the Almighty.' Is it any wonder John collapses! The beloved disciple is privileged with receiving, then sharing the wonder of the person crucified, risen, ascended to glory. There are 27 titles given to Jesus throughout the book of the unveiling. It is also the book which promises the reader and the hearer the blessing of the Lord. Too often it is so easy to by-pass them and be caught up in the spectacular, the imagery and the horror of the judgements and miss the blessing.

Man of sorrows no longer! Jesus is the Lord of glory. Revelation holds the Deity and Humanity of the Lord Jesus in majestic tension. Within its pages we behold the 'Lamb' and realise He is at the same time the Lord God of Hosts. He is shown as the Saviour but also the Judge. His Deity is strongly emphasised by 'I am the Alpha and the Omega' (Revelation 1:8). His Humanity is endorsed in Chapter 22:16: 'I am the root and the descendant of David.' It is this unity of the natures within Christ Jesus which is hard to explain yet vital to faith. It also gives Him the authority, the integrity and the capacity to be the judge of the living and the dead.

History is heading for the apocalypse at a place called Armageddon (Revelation 16:16). There Jesus will be revealed as the Defender of His people. There He becomes the conqueror of Babylon, the false prophet and the antichrist, Death and the Devil. There He is seen as the Lord of Hosts, the warrior. There the radiance of His glory will be seen by all creation. When that happens, a new Age is about to be unveiled.

Maranatha!

The Hill of the Lord
Day 19

Verse. 'The Lord has chosen Zion; he has desired it for his habitation: This is my resting place forever; here I will reside, for I have desired it' Psalm 132:13-14.

God chooses some things which people may consider strange. Why, they wonder, would He set His affections on the descendants of Abraham, Isaac and Jacob? Their amazement includes the land of Israel and the very specific spot called the temple mount. Choose them He did! We are left in no doubt about God's interest in them, and especially 'The Hill'! It is holy ground.

Abraham was promised land for His descendants. Moses was promised a chosen place where God would be worshipped and where offerings would be made (Deuteronomy 12:21). In the reign of David 'The Hill' was possessed. In the time of Solomon the temple for the Lord was built. 1 Kings 8:10 records the moment when the cloud of the presence of the Lord claimed His house. People would have been aware of His presence up to their Babylonian captivity. Ezekiel 8-11 speaks of the Lord's Shekinah glory departing from 'The Hill'.

However, in Isaiah 14:12-14 we read of a spiritual identity called 'Day Star, son of Dawn' or Lucifer in KJV. He wants to usurp and also claim 'the hill of the Lord.' He was the driving force behind the corruption of the worship system and morality of the Israelite priests and people. He was the unseen instigator of the ancient Roman's setting up an image in the temple Jesus attended prior to His crucifixion. Lucifer is the driving force behind Revelation 13 and the setting up of another image in another temple on the same site. Christ foretold this in Matthew 24:15-27 and quoted the prophet Daniel. What the Romans did to the temple of Christ's day was a foretaste of what is yet to happen. It is in Revelation that we have the final scene played out. After these revelations become reality then Daniel's vision will be completed. The Son of Man, the Lord of Glory, smashes the spirit of Babylon and its kingdoms. When that happens the Lord's everlasting Kingdom is realised. He returns to the Hill of His heart's delight.

The psalms have a prophetic delight in the knowledge that the Lord will make Zion His dwelling place once again. Psalm 24 resonates with this as it points to the return of the Lord to His holy place. The psalmist's picturesque language about the gates and doors is rich in symbolism. They are pictured as having been bowed down, broken by despair, neglect, corruption and the presence of evil. You can almost feel the sense of the anguish of 'The Hill' through the description of the gates. It had been defiled and usurped by Lucifer and his associates during the great tribulation. Now those forces had been overthrown, cast down and removed by the returning Lord Jesus. "Come on and celebrate" is the psalmist's prophetic invitation to the gates and ancient doors for the rightful resident returns never more to leave. 'Lift up your heads, O gates! And be lifted up, O ancient doors!' is the beginning of a new and holy time. Is it any wonder then that these structures are called upon to rejoice! The hill has been cleansed and reclaimed.

Psalm 24 describes the One who comes to claim His possession. It is in His capacity as the Lord of Hosts He has come from the battle to claim His prize. He is also the King of glory before whom all will bow. He also is the One who is qualified to rule by His humanity being tested and found pure. He is at the same time the Kinsman/Redeemer of Israel and the Saviour of the World. Now in residence the Lord will govern His kingdom. Here, the nations will come to seek His counsel (Isaiah 2). Here, another psalm will finally and eternally be realised. No longer a place of conflict, or cause for trembling, Zion will then radiate with the joy of the Lord! We are invited to sing today, in faith, the following words: 'Great is the Lord and greatly to be praised in the city of our God. His holy mountain, beautiful in elevation, is the joy of the whole earth, Mount Zion, in the far north, the city of the great King' (Psalm 48:1-2).

Maranatha!

When God Sings Solo
Day 20

Verse: 'The Lord your God is in your midst, a warrior who gives victory; he will rejoice over you with gladness, he will renew you in his love; he will exult over you with loud singing' Zephaniah 3:17.

Surely, this must be one of the most glorious insights into the God who has redeemed us! He who gave creation a [1]song, and will again cause the heavens and earth to [2]sing, is the composer. He is the one who gives us a [3]new song for He has redeemed us. We have much to sing about but He is the One who is the reason for the song. On earth we sing by faith and testimony now. In Heaven we will sing, make music and worship our Lord and Redeemer by sight. Why is there so much song and music from the lips of Christ's people? Because He loves music, melody and song. He gives His people reason to sing.

Yahweh is the original singer! There is, however, only one place where it says He sings. That is our opening verse. Read the context and realise why He sings. He is the warrior Lord who sings to those He has redeemed, those who called upon Him in the midst of the great tribulation. Now, the Lord of Hosts rejoices over His people and sings His delight. Is there any religion which proclaims a God of grace who will one day sing to His people? I know no other!

Do you wonder what this heavenly solo will sound like? We are told that the voice of His judgements are [4]'majestic and as a [5]roaring'. John the apostle heard it as the [6]sound of many waters. Ezekiel had a similar awareness, not so much of the voice but the very [7]sound of the glory of Yahweh. The prophet described it as a fast flowing waterfall. Standing near to such a waterfall a person can be captivated by its overwhelming, enchanting sound. God's voice will have a similar attraction.

Our Lord's song has renewing power. All around will be the smoking rubble of war and earthly cataclysms. People will be in various stages of emotional distress, wonderment and relief. Today we are aware of post–traumatic stress and many hearers of the song will be in that frame of mind. The Lord God of Hosts puts aside His sword and sings a love song. Hearing the sound of His voice and 'drinking in' the words will be rejuvenating to mind, soul, spirit and body. Music can be therapeutic, refreshing, and comforting! When the Saviour sings the people will bow in wonder and rise renewed. Never in all of history or eternity past would there have been such a song.

What is the theme of His song? His beloved ones! He will exult over them with loud singing. This is a song the whole universe will hear. Will this be one of those times when creation joins in? 'Sing, O heavens, for the Lord has done it; shout, O depths of the earth; break forth into singing, O mountains, O forest, and every tree in it! For the Lord has redeemed Jacob, and will be glorified in Israel' (Isaiah 44:23). This is poetic of course but it does give a glimpse of the transformation promised to a world in bondage.

After effects from the Lord of Host's song in the ensuing days are surely expressed in the following verse. 'So the ransomed of the Lord shall return, and come to Zion with singing; everlasting joy shall be upon their heads; they shall obtain joy and gladness, and sorrow and sighing shall flee away' (Isaiah 51:11).

Maranatha!

[1] Job 38:7. [2]Isaiah 44:23. [3]Psalm 40:3. [4]Isaiah 30:30. [5]Jeremiah 25:30. [6]Revelation 1:15.

[7]Ezekiel 43:2.

Sheep, Goats and the King
Day 21

Verse: 'the Lord … is coming to judge the world with righteousness and the peoples with his truth' Psalm 96:13.

Abraham pleaded with Yahweh not to destroy Sodom and Gomorrah. Lot and his family was probably uppermost in Abraham's mind. From initially asking for mercy if 50 righteous could be found Abraham settled for 10 (Genesis 18:23-33). Having made his request he concluded with 'Shall not the Judge of all the earth do what is just?' The word 'judge' described God as a magistrate. This is the first use of the term for God. Ten couldn't be found and so the judicial sentence was carried out. In the future this role of Judge will be undertaken by Jesus. The Father has bestowed it on Him according to John 5:26-27.

A number of judgements will take place on the Lord's return. One of them concerns the Gentile Nations. Jesus highlighted this in His parable of Matthew 25:31-46. Unfortunately, this passage is often wrongly used to motivate people to be active in social justice. Its main emphasis is thereby overlooked through faulty interpretation and application. The parable reveals Jesus setting up His throne of glory as Judge. Before Him will assemble the nations which have survived the various conflicts of the End Times. It is accounting time! It does not refer to individuals. What is the charge the nations have to answer? How they treated the Lord's brethren during the great tribulation time. Their words about what they did or didn't do, will reveal them to be either 'sheep or goats'. How? Because it uncovers the nation's allegiances to either Jesus the Christ or to the anti–Christ. Apparently there is no neutral ground. The question therefore of utmost importance is, 'who are the Brethren of Jesus?

It is natural to understand the term from its use in the Gospels and the book of Acts. When used it points to either the family of Mary and Joseph or to the Nation of Israel (Acts 1`:14. 2:29, 37). Could they also include the 144,000 men from out of the 12 tribes of Israel mentioned in Revelation 7? These were gathered out of every nation for the purpose of sharing the gospel and impending return of the Lord. Either way 'the Brethren' are Jewish. From Matthew's account 'the Brethren' are either cared for or ill-treated. Being a 'sheep nation' would not have been easy during this time. Possibly covertly various branches of Government reached out and ministered to 'my Brethren'. Those called 'goat nations' expressed no such compassion from their Government agencies. In fact, the official policy of the State would have been intent upon destroying 'my Brethren'.

The 'Brethren' who qualify for the 'sheep Nations' are treated unjustly, presumably by the forces loyal to the anti-Christ. However, it is contrary to the particular Nation's wishes. As such, the Nation tends to their welfare whether overtly or covertly. Those within the 'goat Nations' are persecuted, harassed and hounded as an official policy of the State.

This parable has links reaching back to Yahweh's promise to Abram. 'I will make you a great nation … I will bless those who bless you, and the one who curses you I will curse; and in you all the families of the earth shall be blessed' (Genesis 12:2-3). When the Lord divides the sheep and goat nations is this the ultimate fulfilment of the promise to Abram? We understand that for individuals to be saved required a personal commitment to Christ Jesus as Lord, Messiah and Redeemer. In this time of Nation accounting none of that is mentioned or implied. How could a Nation's identity be kept from eternal oblivion? It must flow from the Genesis 12 promise. Those who have blessed Israel (and possibly through helping the 144,000) have in turn been blessed by the Father. How? With an inheritance within the Kingdom of God. The 'sheep Nations' exercised their faith in the Word of God, similar to Abram, and it will be counted to them as righteousness. The 'goat Nations' didn't believe God's Word and were judged as unrighteous. Nothing unrighteous can enter the Kingdom of God therefore they are excluded from it.

Even in the midst of this judgement the power of God's grace will be known. The 'goat Nation' is rejected but there will be individuals from them who are redeemed. This is guaranteed because out of every tribe, language, people and nation there are those who Christ redeemed (Revelation 5:9. 7:9).

Maranatha!

Reflections/study #3.

*Which study aroused your interest the most the past week?

*Have you considered the 1000 year reign of Christ as either literal or spiritual?

*Your insights regarding Jesus being King: Does this apply to His relationship with the Church?

*Do you agree with the concept of what the Lord of hosts wears to battle?

*Have you ever realised our God is the original Singer?

The Judgement Seat of Christ
Day 22

Verse: 'All of us must appear before the judgement seat of Christ, so that each may receive recompense for what has been done in the body, whether good or evil' 2 Corinthians 5:10.

Three major judgements await the coming of the Kingdom of God. Yesterday was one for the Nations. Another before the Great White Throne is mentioned in Revelation 20. Here God opens two books and judges those raised in the second resurrection. This was to sentence them according to their deeds. Salvation was not an option. The third Judgement is mentioned in 2 Corinthians 5:10 and Romans 14:10. This is the Bema of Christ before which the Church must give account. The Bema or tribunal was a portable chair, seat or throne placed on a raised platform. It was from such a throne that Pilate passed sentence upon Jesus (John 19:13). Paul, to the Corinthians, used the Bema concept to distinguish Christ's judgement of the Church from the Great White Throne.

All of us must appear... There are no leave passes or sick notes allowed. This accounting time isn't about salvation. Rather, it is being assessed for faithfulness to our calling in Christ. 'He it is who gave himself for us that he might redeem us from all iniquity and purify for himself a people of his own who are zealous of good deeds' (Titus 2:14). It is easy to understand what the Lord will be weighing in 'the balances.' How do we measure up to His purity requirements? This isn't merely an outward sign. Rather, the Lord sees what the heart stores and motivates, those hidden chambers and mental unwholesome playgrounds where repentance hasn't penetrated.

Also mentioned are 'good deeds.' Again it isn't what we have done for God that counts. It is whether or not we have done what He required of us. Paul used the analogy of running a race in 1 Corinthians 9:24-27 to stress this point. You have to run the race according to the rules, not how you imagine them to be. As runners in the Christian life it isn't first past the post who wins. Everyone is a winner who completes the course according to Christ Jesus' instructions. Those who do their own thing still win but are not crowned with the victor's garland.

However, some special emphases about judgements are placed upon certain ministry areas. Jesus clarified this in the parable of the faithful and unfaithful slaves: 'From everyone to whom much has been given, much will be required; and from the one to whom much has been entrusted, even more will be demanded' (Luke 12:48). This has many applications. Here it concerns leadership. The apostle Peter urged Pastors to exercise their role willingly as God would have them do it (1 Peter 5:2). Leaders in the local churches such as Elders and Deacons are urged to set an example in faith and ministry. Why? Because they will have to give an account of their care to their 'flock.' Another calling specially marked out for judgement is that of Teacher. James 3:1 tells us such people will be judged with greater strictness. Do you understand why? False or glib teaching leads people to a shallow understanding of God's will at best. In the worst scenario it leads to a false understanding of grace, salvation and the second coming. We are not to stray from the Truth, from the holiness of God's calling and the appreciation of His word.

Each of us will give an account not merely about our own personal faith and knowledge: we also have various relationships about which we will be assessed. To mention just a few these will include husbands and wives, parents, children, masters and slaves [business people and workers] and rulers too. Hopefully this may motivate each of us to evaluate how we are living out these relationships from the Bible's teaching. Jesus, as Judge, isn't deaf to the cries of those abused, neglected or exploited by Christians. Read James' letter for a clearer understanding on this very practical matter.

So each may receive recompense ... What that 'May' is, isn't spelt out. Ephesians 6:8 links it to a sowing 'Good' into the lives of others and receiving back from the Lord His blessing! Hebrews 10:32-36 goes into more detail but links it to pursuing and doing 'good' under great difficulties. What cannot be doubted is the fact our Lord takes an interest in what we do, to whom we do it, why we do it and whether or not it brings honour to Him!

Maranatha!

Behold 'The Lamb'
Day 23

Verse: 'These are they who have come out of the great ordeal; they have washed their robes and made them white in the blood of the Lamb' Revelation 7:14.

More titles for and descriptive names of Jesus are used in Revelation than anywhere else.

One name, one title, outstrips them all for the number of times it is used in this epistle. It is 'The Lamb'. John was caught up into Heaven in a vision to hear about and write down the age's final days. When he is there he is confronted by a closed and sealed book. This would appear to be the one Daniel sealed according to Daniel 12:4. He didn't know its contents and it would not be revealed 'until the time of the end'. That time had arrived. In anticipation the apostle watched to see who could unlock the seals. It would seem that various ones where considered but failed the test.

John wept bitterly. One of the twenty-four Elders spoke to John saying that the 'Lion of Judah, Root of David had proven worthy.' Through tears John beheld the One, the only One, who has the authority to open it. Before him stood, not a 'Lion' but 'a Lamb standing as if it had been slaughtered…' (Revelation 5:6). This was Jesus Christ, the Lamb of God with scars that testified to the savagery of the contest surrounding the cross. The victory gained over Death, Sin, and the Devil by His Righteousness before the Law and His Father gave Him the right to open the sealed book. Now began the final countdown of prophetic history.

In plain, symbolic and also poetic language the real nature of evil is unmasked. Now its intentions over the centuries has been forced into the open. Those corrupt spiritual forces make their final effort to establish their rule. There is a dragon, who is the devil, plus the anti–Christ, the false prophet who is also a miracle worker. God hating, lustful, power-mad nations also join together to oppose the coming Kingdom of God under the banner of Babylon. This apostate world religion in league with a One World government have as their aim to defeat, then destroy 'The Lamb' slain from before the foundation of the world (Revelation 13:8). The conqueror of Calvary will be the opposing force at Armageddon. On the cross the Lamb took away the sin of the world and the Father's judgement on it. Now He will remove all that opposes the Kingdom of God and His holiness. The anguish of those in the Kingdom of Darkness is summed up in the following words. 'Fall on us and hide us from the face of the one seated on the throne and from the wrath of the Lamb' (Revelation 6:16).

Contrasted with that is the song sung by countless angels, the living creatures and the elders in glory. 'Worthy is the Lamb that was slaughtered to receive power and wealth and wisdom and might and honour and glory and blessing' (Revelation 5:12). They are joined by a multitude that no one could count. From every nation, tribe, people and language group these redeemed will join in with their song. They heard the Gospel and accept Jesus as their Lord and Saviour and were martyred. The Lamb holds them in great favour: 'The Lamb at the centre of the throne will be their shepherd, and will guide them to springs of the water of life, and God will wipe away every tear from their eyes' (Revelation 7:16). Their testimony in life and death is that they conquered the dragon by the blood of the Lamb (Revelation12:11).

Today's devotional closes with another Hallelujah chorus ringing in our hearts. This is the final description of the Lamb. 'Hallelujah! For the Lord our God the Almighty reigns. Let us rejoice and exult and give him glory, for the marriage supper of the Lamb has come, and his bride has made herself ready…' (Revelation 19:6-7). It is as the Lamb of God He redeemed us. It is as the Lamb of God Jesus conquers. It is as the Lamb slaughtered, risen and victorious He invites us to the great celebration which is coming. It will be to the Lamb we will sing. To the Lamb we will bow and worship. Until then it is to the Lamb here and now we must honour, serve and worship.

Maranatha!

Heralds of Apostasy
Day 24

Verse: 'Brothers and sisters, stand firm and hold fast to the traditions that you were taught by us, either by word of mouth or by our letter' 2 Thessalonians 2:15.

The greatest threat to the life of the early church was not Caesar and his legions. It was through Satan's infiltration of smooth talking false teachers. The Galatian letter unmasks some. Colossians warns about others. John's letters to the seven churches stresses the need to be vigilant. Perhaps the shortest letter written by Jude holds the greatest warning. 'Certain intruders have stolen in among you ... who pervert the grace of our God into licentiousness and deny our only Master and Lord, Jesus Christ.'

The Devil has a superb network of undercover agents. Their commission is to lead men and women away from the truth of God's Word. Then they pervert the message of Christ and the cross through unbelief, partial truth, bad exegesis and immorality. This lays the groundwork into acceptance of the counterfeit religion of the Antichrist. Both the New and Old Testaments unmask these undercover agents. They are called 'false teachers, false prophets and false apostles'. Paul calls them 'deceitful workers, disguising themselves as apostles of Christ' (2 Corinthians 11:13). God is especially angry against these corrupters of His word, His salvation, His Son, His people and His name.

A frightful insight as to where false teaching leads to is found in 2 Thessalonians 2. 'As to the coming of our Lord Jesus Christ ...that day will not come unless the rebellion comes first and the lawless one is revealed'. Ultimately the path takes a person to the one Jesus said would appear 'in his own name' (John 5:43). This is the man who epitomises all those who were his forerunners such as Antiochus Epiphany who is alluded to in Daniel 11. The word 'rebellion' is from the Greek 'apostasia' and means a revolt, a defection, a falling away. There is a standard from which false teachers take a person and causes them to fall into apostasy. It is, 'The faith that was once for all entrusted to the saints' (Jude 3). The seriousness of this can be read in the letter to the Galatians. Paul said such teachers are cursed. Why? Because they preach another [so-called] gospel thereby teaching an entirely different Jesus.

The effects of these saboteurs of the Faith is shown in the seven churches of Revelation. In four out of the seven there is a toleration of unbelief, immorality, idolatry and occultism. The church of Laodicea highlights the tragedy of apostasy. That congregation was outwardly prosperous, lukewarm spirituality and worst of all, Jesus is left outside. That means the congregation is no longer in the Body of Christ. The people merely form a religious club. They seem to be a people blind to the truth, poor in spiritual riches, naked, for they have not the garments of righteousness. However, to the Churches of Revelation there was still hope. The Lord offered mercy on the condition of repentance. Rejecting His offer would open the way to judgement.

A key word associated with believing the Gospel is 'continue' in it. This requires perseverance. The reality of a personal faith is summed up in these words. Remaining true, committed and faithful means a believer must 'stand firm and hold fast' to God's word. To stand firm requires a strong foothold on an unmoveable foundation. The parable of the two builders in Matthew 7 speaks to this. *Hold fast*, in the verse for today, has the idea of a strong grip. Jesus Christ holds His people in His hand, what do we hold? The opening verse uses 'tradition'. That's something handed down. Jesus referred to it in John 5:39 when He said the Scriptures pointed to Him. Peter wrote that tradition is the prophetic message confirmed in the person of Jesus (2Peter 1:16-21).

Tied to 'continuing' and ''standing firm' is the 'contend for the faith' mentioned by Jude. Not every believer is equipped to debate or refute, but all are called upon to uphold the Name and teaching of Jesus. In whatever era of history or country Christians live they are to work out those three issues. It isn't easy now, but in the time of the great apostasy it becomes a life and death issue. The apostles could see the seeds of the apostasy being sown in their lifetime. In his final letter Paul warns Timothy of emerging trends and the price the faithful will pay to stand firm and continue in the faith (2Timothy

4:1-8). At the same time he reminds the reader the reward from the Lord is the crown of righteousness. What is the fate of Satan's undercover agents? They are 'cut down and thrown into the fire' (Matthew 7:20).

Maranatha!

Jerusalem, no longer Forsaken
Day 25

Verse: 'You (Jerusalem) shall no more be termed Forsaken, and your land shall no more be termed Desolate; but you shall be called My Delight is in her' Isaiah 62:4.

Jacob's children are 'chained' to Jerusalem and the land of Israel. Through nearly two thousand years of dispossession and oppression their Passover lament was 'Next year in Jerusalem.' Nations over centuries have ravaged the city whilst today it is still a centre for international dilemma and anxiety. Jesus wept over it. At the same time He knew it had a brighter destiny (Matthew 23:37-39).

The story of Jerusalem is a love story between the Covenant keeping Lord and a fickle and faithless people. Why would the Lord endure such unfaithfulness and disobedience? Answer: 'For the gifts and calling of God are irrevocable' (Romans 11:29.) We should take heart from this and the Lord's patience and discipline on Jerusalem. Why? Because the Church isn't any better behaved! Also, many of us are or have been wanderers from the 'straight and narrow path'. We enjoy stressing the wonder of 'nothing being able to separate us from the Love of God' in Romans 8:35-39. On what do we base such an awesome hope? The faithfulness of the Lord! The apostle Paul gives an unequalled illustration in Romans 9-11 to this awesome truth. He used God's dealing with Israel as a testimony to the promise inherent in 'nothing can separate us' from His grace.

Jerusalem has a great destiny foreshadowed in Scripture. Why then did Jesus weep over it? Because He knew what was in the 'wings' of their history. Their obstinate, unbelieving heart and the hatred of the Gentile Nations would bring calamity before fulfilment. But the suffering Servant's love for His city knew the prophetic writings. Did you grasp the significance of two words in the key verse? *'No more'*. When you read the prophets take note of these and similar words such as 'never' 'never again'. They are a statement of the Suffering Servant having redeemed Israel. Jesus, as their King, returns to deliver the city from destruction as it faced in Zechariah 14.

Isaiah pictured the Lord God as restless. 'For Zion's sake I will not keep silent, and for Jerusalem's sake I will not rest, until her vindication shines out like the dawn, and her salvation like a burning torch' (Isaiah 62:1). The Lord waits impatiently for it to be time. His delay ensures all the preparations will be complete. Isaiah's picture of the Lord God's plan for Jerusalem is to make 'her a crown of beauty' ... and a 'royal diadem in the hand of ... God.' This will not be a secret affair. The God of Heaven will vindicate His choice in placing His name in that city. Forever!

We live in a World of instant news. We read of the volatile situations in the Middle East and scratch our heads how things will ever work out. The United Nations under the influence of Arab nations and their Islamic religion deny Israel's right to the Land and to Jerusalem. This must surely be one of the most historically ignorant decisions ever made. It not only denies Biblical testimony but also secular historical records. Once again we are witnessing the animosity of the Gentile world to Israel. Once again we understand the power of the god of this world as he blinds their minds to truth. What a challenge to the promises of God regarding the land, the people and the capital of Israel. His sadness over such stupidity and where it will lead is written in psalm 2 (see days 4, 6).

Isaiah 62 is the greatest proverbial slap in the face to those denying the right of Israel to exist. This chapter uses strong, beautiful and uncompromising words from the lips of God through the pen of the prophet. The nations will see His vindication of and His glory in this city. It will be a crown of beauty, a royal diadem in God's hand. Jerusalem will be called 'Hephzibah', meaning God's delight. This city which makes the world tremble will be renowned worldwide and the people will be holy, redeemed! "I am about to create Jerusalem as a joy, and its people as a delight. I will rejoice in Jerusalem" (Isaiah 65:18-19). No longer forsaken.

Maranatha!

The Epiphany of Christ
Day 26

Verse: 'While we wait for the blessed hope and the manifestation [epiphany] of the glory of our great God and Saviour, Jesus Christ' Titus 2:13.

Scattered throughout the prophetic work of Isaiah are portraits of the promised Messiah. They cover [a] His birth, [b] His family line, [c] His character, [d] His substitutionary death, [e] His avenging return and [f] His reign from Jerusalem. In chapter 9 Isaiah likens the Messiah's appearance as a great light. Matthew links this to Jesus when He moved to Capernaum. Notice, the emphasis on the people seeing 'a great light' and that 'light had dawned'.

Jesus said He is the Light of the world and to walk with Him is to be delivered from Darkness. When Jesus was born at Bethlehem the word used in Titus[1] speaks of His epiphany. His appearance at that time was to secure the salvation of men and women. That's the story of the cross. Christ's appearance is testimony to the goodness and kindness of God[2]. What He taught, endured and accomplished in redeeming believers must be acknowledged. This is done with the lips of praise. A lifestyle renouncing the realm of darkness and reflecting the 'light of Christ' is also required. In the letters to Timothy and Titus there are a number of reasons why Christians are 'lights in a dark and evil world'.

Being thankful for redemption and justification[3] head the list. Being heirs[4] of glory is another factor. Looking forward to a crown of righteousness when Jesus' 'epiphany' happens is also highly motivational. 'Keep the commandment without spot or blame until the manifestation [epiphany] of our Lord Jesus Christ, which He will bring about at the right time…'[5]. When is that 'right time'? God alone knows. That is why a key word of faith is [6]'wait'! Waiting is not being idle, it means expressing our relationship as 'light bearers' by lifestyle and message. This was uppermost in Paul's final letter as he faced death under Caesar Nero. Being assured of Christ's epiphany the apostle urges Timothy to keep on proclaiming the message of the cross. He was not to take account of whether the situation in society was favourable or not. Timothy, and therefore those who belong to and serve the Lord, must do it with patience.

During the week leading to His crucifixion, Jesus was moved to tears by His nation's blindness and hardness of heart. He could see the coming destruction which took place in A.D. 66-70. He knew that the nation would be scattered and persecuted. Even when they returned to their own land they would endure a great tribulation. Jesus also saw beyond all this horror and made a wonderful announcement about them and His appearing. "I tell you, you will not see me again until you say 'Blessed is the one who comes in the name of the Lord'" (Matthew 23:39). When Jesus appears the records tell us it will be with a brilliant expression of Heaven's Light! That is, Himself. Accompanied by His angels described in Hebrews as 'servants of fire' His epiphany will be awesome. Is it any wonder the term 'lightning' is used to describe how the sky lights up at Christ's return! Scriptures tells us the ungodly will mourn but the believers will lift up their heads and rejoice. Another matter to be dealt with is the man of Lawlessness who had scourged Israel and others, especially Christ's followers. The sheer brilliance of Christ's person combined with the sword of His mouth, will destroy Satan's counterfeit ruler.

Three words are intertwined with the return of Christ Jesus. They are, Apocalypse, Parousia and Epiphany. Each combine to give us an understanding of the Person we call Lord and Saviour, Jesus, Son of God. We will behold Him in His unveiled Glory. His presence will be with us as Lord of lords and King of kings. In that presence no darkness can exist for His epiphany will be the Light of lights. The brilliance of Christ's presence will cause the sun to disappear. The radiance of His Apocalypse and Parousia will be our experience eternally (Revelation 21:23-24).

Maranatha!

[a] Isaiah 9:1-7. [b] Isaiah 11:1. [c] Isaiah 42. [d] Isaiah 53. [e] Isaiah 63. [f] Isaiah 2:1-4.

[1] Titus 3:4. [2] Titus 3:4. [3] Titus 3:7. [4] Titus 3:7. [5] 1 Timothy 6:14. [6] Titus 2:13.

The Chariots of Clouds
Day 27

Verse: '(Jesus) was lifted up, and a cloud took him out of their sight…Two men in white robes stood by them. They said, "Men of Galilee, why do you stand looking up toward heaven? This Jesus…will come in the same way as you saw him go into heaven"' Acts 1:9-11.

Under oath Jesus said He was the Son of Man who would come with the clouds of Heaven. This is the prophecy of Daniel 7:13. He signed His own death warrant with that. He was charged with blasphemy. Reading Matthew's and Luke's account we discern three grounds for this. All of them converge on the fact that He was claiming to be Emmanuel, God with us.

What were the three aspects that made the Nation's leaders demand Pilate issue death by crucifixion? i) Jesus claimed to be the Son of Man. ii) He admitted He was the Son of God. iii) He associated Himself with the coming on the clouds of heaven. Aligning Himself with the titles of 'Son of Man' and 'Son of God' was enough to guarantee the death penalty. However, it is easy to overlook the importance of number three.

Moses and the Psalmists identified clouds with the very presence of Yahweh. He made Himself known on mount Horeb in clouds of deepest darkness. He led Israel through the wilderness in a pillar of cloud by day and a pillar of fire at night. When the Tabernacle, and then the Temple were complete, God made His presence known by a cloud. The High Priest and others soon realised the implications when the man from Nazareth linked Himself to the clouds. It was a comparison to God that was too much to bear.

In 'Captured by Calvary' I wrote if there isn't any resurrection the Sanhedrin was correct. Praise God for the resurrection's affirmation of Jesus as the Christ, the Son of God. Forty days later on the Mount of Olives Jesus is associated with clouds again. Acts 1:9, 'As they were watching, he was lifted up, and a cloud took him out of their sight.'

When the two men in white said those words did any of the disciples understand their significance? Over and over again Scripture identifies the Yahweh of the Old Testament as the Jesus of the New Testament. What a wonderful privilege we have to unashamedly confess that this Jesus is our Lord and Saviour.

Notice the emphasis of the angels: '*This Jesus...*' is the Bethlehem warrior baby who became the prophet from Galilee. *This Jesus* who became the crucified servant has risen, victor over the tomb. *This Jesus* is the Lord who has ascended to His Father's presence. *This Jesus*, not another, *this Jesus* with the scars from the cross will return. 'He will come in the same way as you saw him go...' How was that? Visible, tangible and from the Mount of Olives in clouds.

Can anything be more specific? Wiped out are such teachings as a spiritual, unseen return or a replacement Christ and certainly returning to any place but the Mount of Olives. The prophet Zechariah foresaw this event. In chapter 14:3-4 he paints an end time scenario: 'Then the Lord will go forth and fight against those nations as when he fights on a day of battle. On that day his feet shall stand on the Mount of Olives...' Can you see the link? The Lord of Hosts in the Old Testament is confirmed as the Jesus of the New.

What the disciples saw made a lasting impression. John the writer of Revelation had the scene burned into his mind. When he came to write the Revelation the reader is gripped by his association of Christ's return and clouds. Revelation 1:7,'Look! He is coming with the clouds; every eye will see him, even those who pierced him; and on his account all the tribes of the earth will wail.' Do you have any idea as to why the tribes of the earth will be lamenting the return of Christ Jesus? It will be judgement time.

To speculate as to how every eye will see Him is a bit of a mind tease but the 'How' isn't spelt out. From other readings you will understand there is a lot of activity preceding this coming. In one of His final discourses Jesus gave this instruction; 'Now when these things begin to take place, stand up and raise your heads, because your redemption is drawing near.' (Luke 21:28)

Maranatha!

Universal Restoration Begun
Day 28

Verse: 'Jesus…must remain in heaven until the time of universal restoration that God announced long ago through his holy prophets' Acts 3:21.

It caught the man's eye. Rusty, derelict, smothered by blackberry bushes and home of vermin the car was apparently worthless. He collected all he could and took it home. Years later the same car took to the road in pristine condition. Restored to more than its former glory the car aroused admiration and delight! Such an amazing transformation underscores the Greek word for '*restored*' in the verse above. It also describes the word used in Acts 1:6, 'Lord is this the time when you will *restore* (emphasis added) the kingdom to Israel?' The apostles knew their Bible. They had sat with, walked with and listened to Jesus as He shared wonderful insights into this Kingdom.

Peter took the opportunity through the healing of the crippled beggar to share about the Messiah with the gathered crowd. Although the Nation had authorised His crucifixion, forgiveness was still offered by the risen Jesus. Also, He would bring the times of refreshing promised by the prophets. The word picture behind 'refreshing' is one of being cool after the heat of the day. For Israel it will be a coming out of the furnace of Gentile affliction and captivity and into their fulfilment of God's promises. This can only take place through national repentance. What was the national sin needing attention? This was rejection of Jesus as their Saviour and King through unbelief towards that which Moses and the prophets wrote about the coming Messiah. Peter offered the rulers of the people an excuse for their treatment of Jesus. It was out of ignorance and was covered by Christ's prayer "Father, forgive them; for they do not know what they are doing".

Peter also included in the time of refreshing the promised universal restoration. This would include, but go beyond, the restoration of the Kingdom to Israel. What will be 'restored'? This requires some knowledge of what has been lost, corrupted, stolen and vandalised. The answers are in the records kept from Genesis to Malachi. We know what Adam lost for his descendants, a 'walk in the garden' with the Lord God (Genesis 3). That will be restored when Jesus Christ returns. Through Humankind's wickedness described in Genesis 6:1-7 Creation was corrupted and condemned to bondage. When the Lord sets foot on the earth Creation's groaning and captivity will end (Isaiah 11:1-9). The result of this will be seen in longevity of life once more for those born in the thousand year reign. Ultimately, it means the new heavens and the new earth.

Included in all of this is the restoration of the Kingdom of Israel under the rule of the Kingdom of God. The land of Canaan was promised to Abraham's offspring, through Isaac and Jacob (Genesis 12:3, 7). Unfaithfulness to the covenants led to their judgement and dispersion. Even today, though a Nation, they only occupy part of the land promised. The promise has not been annulled. God said to King David 'Your house and your kingdom shall be made sure forever before me; your throne shall be established forever' (2 Samuel 7:16). Because Jesus is of the human lineage of David He will sit upon that throne. As much as some don't like the idea, there is a bonding between the Davidic Kingdom and the Kingdom of God. Consider 1 Chronicles 17:1-15, with special emphasis in verses 11-14.

The last one to sit on the throne of the Kingdom of Israel in the line of David was Zedekiah. Ezekiel explains why the Almighty and everlasting God has kept His covenant with a proud and obstinate Nation. It is for 'His Name's sake.' All nations shall understand Yahweh keeps His word with the underlying and overarching purpose being summed up 65 times in Ezekiel with the words "Then they will know that I am the Lord."

Vacated but not abandoned, the throne waits for the return of the Lord Jesus. Zechariah 14:1-9 declares the returning Lord will set foot upon the Mount of Olives, becoming King over all the earth. His throne will be in Jerusalem (Ezekiel 43:7). The prophet's last words are 'the name of the city from that time on shall be, Yahweh Shammah, 'The Lord is there.'

Maranatha!

Reflection/Study#4

*Do you see any difference between the 'Bema' of Christ and the Great White Throne? (day 22).

*What are your insights into the 'restraining force' which is in operation at the moment? (day 24).

*Does the literal city of Jerusalem have a future in God's purposes?

*With so many past and future counterfeits, how is the true Jesus recognized?

*You pick from the past week's devotions.

Clues to Christ's Return
Day 29

Verse: 'When you see all these things, you know that he is near, at the very gates' Matthew 24:33.

Clues are strategically placed throughout Scripture concerning the first and second comings of Jesus. The Lord hasn't left the world in ignorance of His purposes. Some are plainly stated such as the place of the Messiah's birth being Bethlehem. Others are mixed in with some other details and need careful sifting. Jesus also gave a clue as to the resurrection when He likened it to Jonah's experience in the giant fish (Matthew 12:38-40). Therefore we should not be surprised by our Lord's planting certain clues to His return for us to consider.

In Matthew 24 He provocatively initiates a discussion with His disciples. After attending the temple they boasted about the glory of the temple. The Lord prophesied such glory would become rubble. Later, on the Mount of Olives, the twelve asked three questions: 'Tell us, when will this be, and what will be the sign of your coming and of the end of the age?' (Matthew 24:3) Let us have a brief look at the second of their questions. Whilst no one knows the exact time, there will be an intensive moral and spiritual breakdown as in the days of Noah. This will give rise to massive persecution of believers. Centuries have come and gone with varying degrees of persecution, moral breakdown and heresy. They are glimpses to the Great Tribulation. An increase in natural disasters and signs in the Heavens plus many, many false Messiahs makes for troubling times. Revelation also gives us insights into Yahweh's judgements which happen during this period.

Matthew puts five parables together in chapters 24-25 all dealing with aspects of Christ Jesus' return. They are the judgement on 'the faithful and the unfaithful slave': The 10 Bridesmaids, The Talents, The Sheep and goats. One parable about the 'Fig tree' is of interest to us. Being a symbol of Israel, the Lord used the Gentile Nations treatment of them as a 'clue' to His nearness. The slumber of Israel's spiritual winter will one day give way to their spiritual summer. Such a momentous event is graphically portrayed in Ezekiel's vision of the valley of dry bones in chapter 37. Much speculation about this has and will take place but the prophets are in no doubt that it will happen. Isaiah 49:26b is a fine summary of why it will happen, 'then all flesh shall know that I am the Lord your Saviour, and your Redeemer, the Mighty One of Jacob.'

Further clues lie in both Testaments, pointing to the return of the Lord Jesus. While they may be debated and variously interpreted the issue is ultimately do we believe what is written? Unbelief will cause a spiritual sleeping sickness and thereby slothfulness in worship and lifestyle. Our Lord and Saviour called His followers to 'keep awake', 'understand', and 'be ready'. These are states of mind which underpin personal behaviour and motivation. Our love for the Lord permeates what we do or don't do consciously and subconsciously. So it will be for those alive in the time of Christ's return.

One of the most startling and much debated clues is the destiny of the Church. Before Israel can begin to fulfil its calling in the last days, the Body of Christ must be reunited with Its Head. That is one of the significances of the Rapture when we will meet the Lord in the 'air'. (see day 2). History's final seven years is underway. As Jesus said about that time, "when these things begin to take place, stand up and raise your heads, because your redemption is drawing near" (Luke 21:28).

Maranatha!

Eyes of Fire
Day 30.

Verse: 'To the angel of the church in Thyatira write: These are the words of the Son of God, who has eyes like a flame of fire, and whose feet are like burnished bronze' Revelation 2:18.

Those eyes which wept over Jerusalem and expressed affection to little children have become flame throwers. Jesus, as the suffering servant had eyes which beheld the lost, the exploited and prisoners of hopelessness. His eyes expressed His mission to rescue, redeem and restore a sin enslaved world. Now, in Revelation, His eyes blaze with wrath against rampant ungodliness and oppression of His people. It is said that eyes express the character of the soul, Christ's eyes will, at that time, burn with justice fuelled by holiness.

The description of the Son of Man in Revelation chapter 1 must be the most awesome within Scripture. If it caused the apostle to faint what would it have done to us? This unveiling of the crucified Jesus as the Lord of Glory took John, and takes us, on a journey of understanding the 'fire.' In chapter 2 those eyes are fixed upon the church in Thyatira. That fellowship was tolerant of sexually promiscuous people, shared in idolatry and was interested about learning Satan's 'deep things.' As the Son of God, Jesus searches their hearts and minds with His penetrating eyes of fire. Judgement begins at the Church according to 1 Peter 4:17 and is a warning to the ungodly. Those eyes of fire reappear in Revelation 19. Here they turn upon the Nations for their hostility towards Yahweh's person, people and principles.

For seven years the depravation and desecration wrought by the man of Lawlessness took place. Aided and abetted by his counterfeit miracle worker, the false prophet, the Anti-Christ mustered an international army to destroy the Lord Jesus' name and people. This begins in the plain of Meggido. Whichever way you put together the various passages about this event, one thing stands out. It is a momentous, awe-inspiring spectacle.

The Lord of Hosts could have simply rained fire from heaven to achieve His purposes. What is described is for all to realise, now and at that time, this is none other than the Lord's doing. In Matthew 24 Jesus painted a picture of this event with words. He describes a shaking of the heavens and the Son of Man riding the clouds in power and glory. From the east across to the west Jesus' return is as lightning in a dark sky, eye catching in brilliance, heart stopping in its purpose. 2 Thessalonians 1 says the Lord returns in flaming fire, with mighty angels. No longer the despised and rejected One, He comes in glory befitting the warrior Lord. He rode into Jerusalem on the foal of a donkey, a sign of peace, as Israel's King. He was rejected and crucified. Now, He returns on the white horse, as the warrior Lord, accompanied by His angels. He comes to claim the throne and become King of kings and Lord of Lords.

Angels accompanying Him have other tasks than to fight. One part of their mission is given in Matthew 24:31, 'He will send out his angels with a loud trumpet call, and they will gather his elect from the four winds, and from one end of heaven to the other.' Another is found in the parables of Matthew 13. They are the reapers who collect the 'weeds' planted by the enemy of Christ. They also separate the evil from the righteous at the end of the age.

Revelation 19:11-16 pictures Jesus going into battle with this sword, similar to a large one used by the ancient Thracians. The Lord exchanged the former two-edged sword of His mouth for this other style. The sword in Hebrews 4:12 had the power to convert. The Sword in Revelation only had the power to condemn. Jesus engages the enemy by Himself. This isn't hand to hand combat. It is the testimony of the power of His word. Wrath will blaze through the fire in His eyes while His breath consumes those arrayed against Him.

Maranatha!

All Things New
Day 31

Verse: 'The one who was seated on the throne said, "See, I am making all things new"' Revelation 21:5.

We live in an amazing universe. Astronomers keep finding new stars and planets which raise questions and tease their minds. However, all its mysteries and beauty have a used by date. Scripture indicates that this time is much closer than what scientists predict. Within its covers there are some vivid descriptions of the passing of creation and the bringing in of the new. 'In the beginning, Lord, you founded the earth, and the heavens are the work of your hands; they will perish, but you remain; they will all wear out like clothing; like a cloak you will roll them up, and like clothing they will be changed. But you are the same, and your years never end.' Hebrews 1:10-12.

A need for a new creation is apparent due to the old being polluted and put in bondage by Adam's treason (Romans 8:19-22). We all share in this bondage and sinful contamination because he is our Federal Head (Romans 5:12-21). Satan's rebellion brought death and decay upon the Creation initially pronounced 'good!' It will groan until it is made new. The cross secured forgiveness and cleansing for us but we know that within us the old nature grumbles and groans (Galatians 5:16-17. Romans 7:14-25). Even through the millennium reign this carnal nature exists. What Revelation 20 depicts as the final rebellious act indicates sin was operative even in this wonderful time. God's great white throne of judgement is the finale to the old creation.

Fire is the hallmark of God's holiness expressed in acceptance as Elijah knew in 1 Kings 18 on Mount Carmel. Fire also indicates the Lord's holy wrath when it consumed Nadab and Abihu for their wilfulness (Leviticus 10). Fire will consume this old creation for it cannot hold the unfiltered holiness of the Almighty. In the new creation the Triune God's holiness will be seen in all His majestic beauty. There is no way any of us could endure such glory for a moment if we were not made new and clothed in the righteousness of Christ. The important and unchanging message we have is summed up by Peter: we have been given a new birth into a living hope. We have been granted an inheritance which is imperishable, undefiled and unfading in heaven. This and so much more is the result of the Christ of Calvary's triumph (1 Peter 1).

In this new creation a person is required also to be made new. Here again is the wonder of God's grace and the power of Christ's substitutionary death. 2 Corinthians 5:17 says putting our life into Jesus' hands caused us to become a new creation. Our bodies still have to undergo a transforming makeover which is promised in 1 Corinthians 15. Without the 'twinkling of an eye' experience there would be no way of sharing in the new creation. At that moment our body of death is put away and we have a new body fit for glory. We are informed from Philippians 3:21 it will be conformed to the body of His (Christ's) glory.

The Almighty God brings in His new creation by removing the old. Words used to describe this include, destroying it because it is wearing out, rolling it up (Hebrews 1:10-11), shaking it and removing it (Hebrews 12:27). All this seems to be the preparation for the final act when the heavens and the earth are dissolved by fire. When that takes place the promise of Jesus in Revelation 21:5 takes effect, "See, I am making all things new."

Until then may we heed the words 2 Peter 3:11-13. 'Since all these things are to be dissolved … what sort of persons ought you to be in leading lives of holiness and godliness, waiting for and hastening the coming of the day of God, because of which the heavens will be set ablaze and dissolved, and the elements will melt with fire? But, in accordance with His promise, we wait for new heavens and a new earth where righteousness is at home.'

Maranatha!
Until then,
'The Lord bless you and keep you; (The Father)
The Lord make His face shine upon you, and be gracious to you; (The Son)
The Lord lift up His countenance upon you, and give you peace.' (The Holy Spirit) Numbers 6:24-26.

Reflection/study #5

*What other clues can you share about the Lord's return?

*The description of Jesus with fire in His eyes – how does that resonate with you?

*The Christian faith rests upon the unique revelation of God. How do you handle the mystery of mysteries, God the Father, the Son and the Holy Spirit? Deuteronomy 6:4, Matthew 28:19.

*Your final thoughts about these 31 day Devotionals.

Behold He Comes...

Behold He comes...
    No longer wrapped in swaddling cloth
        He's dressed in heavenly armour!
    No longer the meek and mild
        He's burning with righteous anger!
    No longer the suffering One
        He's now the Sovereign Avenger!

Behold He comes...
    He rides upon a chariot of clouds.
    He shatters Death's foul shroud.
    He comes with trumpet loud.

Behold He comes...
    He, the promises to fulfil.
    He, His righteousness instil.
    He, judgments to distil.

Behold He comes...
    He displays God's holy sovereignty.
    He destroys Satan's duplicity.
    He removes all human iniquity.

Behold He comes...
        He, the long expected One.
        He, the risen glorious Son.
        He, the Redeemer, has come!
            We call Him Lord.
            We call Him Saviour.
            We call Him Jesus!
                  He is the Warrior Lord.
                  He is the Lord of Hosts.
                  He is the King of kings!

©Ray Hawkins

www.ingramcontent.com/pod-product-compliance
Lightning Source LLC
Chambersburg PA
CBHW070549300426
44113CB00011B/1842